The History of Family Business, 1850–2000

Prepared for the Economic History Society by

Andrea Colli
Università Commerciale Luigi Bocconi, Milan

CAMBRIDGE
UNIVERSITY PRESS

PUBLISHED BY THE PRESS SYNDICATE OF THE UNIVERSITY OF CAMBRIDGE
The Pitt Building, Trumpington Street, Cambridge CB2 1RP, United Kingdom

CAMBRIDGE UNIVERSITY PRESS
The Edinburgh Building, Cambridge, CB2 2RU, UK
40 West 20th Street, New York, NY 10011-4211, USA
477 Williamstown Road, Port Melbourne, VIC 3207, Australia
Ruiz de Alarcón 13, 28014 Madrid, Spain
Dock House, The Waterfront, Cape Town 8001, South Africa

http://www.cambridge.org

© The Economic History Society 2003

First published 2003

Printed in the United Kingdom at the University Press, Cambridge

Typeface Plantin 10/12.5 pt   *System* LaTeX 2_ε [TB]

A catalogue record for this book is available from the British Library

ISBN 0 521 80028 5 hardback
ISBN 0 521 80472 8 paperback

The History of Family Business, 1850–2000

In this new textbook, Andrea Colli gives a historical and comparative perspective on family business, examining through time the different relationships within family businesses and among family enterprises, inside different political and institutional contexts. He compares the performance of family businesses with that of other economic organisations, and looks at how these enterprises have contributed to the evolution of contemporary industrial capitalism. Central to his discussion are the reasons for both the decline and persistence of family business, how it evolved historically, the different forms it has taken over time, and how it has contributed to the growth of single economies. The book summarises previous research into family business, and situates many aspects of family business – such as their strategies, contribution, failure, and decline – in an economic, social, political, and institutional context. It will be of key interest to students of economic history and business studies.

ANDREA COLLI is Assistant Professor in Economic History at the Università Commerciale Luigi Bocconi, Milan. He is the author of *Legami di ferro* (1998). Has also written with Franco Amatori a book on Italian industrial history (*Impresa e industria in Italia dall'Unità ad oggi*, 1999) and a history of Italian small business (*I volti di Proteo*, 2002).

New Studies in Economic and Social History

Edited for the Economic History Society by
Maurice Kirby
Lancaster University

This series, specially commissioned by the Economic History Society, provides a guide to the current interpretations of the key themes of economic and social history in which advances have recently been made or in which there has been significant debate.

In recent times economic and social history has been one of the most flourishing areas of historical study. This has mirrored the increasing relevance of the economic and social sciences both in a student's choice of career and in forming a society at large more aware of the importance of these issues in their everyday lives. Moreover, specialist interests in business, agricultural, and welfare history, for example, have themselves burgeoned and there has been an increased interest in the economic development of the wider world. Stimulating as these scholarly developments have been for the specialist, the rapid advance of the subject and the quantity of new publications make it difficult for the reader to gain an overview of particular topics, let alone the whole field.

New Studies in Economic and Social History is intended for students and their teachers. It is designed to introduce them to fresh topics and to enable them to keep abreast of recent writing and debates. All the books in the series are written by a recognised authority in the subject, and the arguments and issues are set out in a critical but unpartisan fashion. The aim of the series is to survey the current state of scholarship, rather than to provide a set of pre-packaged conclusions.

The series has been edited since its inception in 1968 by Professors M. W. Flinn, T. C. Smout and L. A. Clarkson, and is currently edited by Professor Maurice Kirby. From 1968 it was published by Macmillan as Studies in Economic History, and after 1974 as Studies in Economic and Social History. Since 1995 New Studies in Economic and Social History has been published on behalf of the Economic History Society by Cambridge University Press. This new series includes some of the titles previously published by Macmillan as well as new titles, and reflects the ongoing development throughout the world of this rich seam of history.

For a full list of titles in print, please see the end of the book.

Contents

Introduction

This book focuses on family business in historical and comparative perspective. Its main aim is to examine through time the evolution of family businesses against varying political and institutional contexts, and to evaluate the performance of family firms in comparison with other forms of business organisations. The ultimate aim is to highlight the contribution of family firms to the evolution of contemporary industrial capitalism. Today, the concept of family business has partially lost its association with the negative notions of backwardness, paternalism, primitive technology, simple organisational structures, and commercial and distributional weakness. Despite the competitive advantages accruing to capital-intensive industries from technology, scale and scope economies, horizontal and vertical integration, and the enlistment of professional managers, since the early 1970s the evolution of knowledge-based industries has emphasised the role of small and medium-sized family businesses. Even if globalisation substantially reaffirmed the key role of the large corporation (Chandler and Hikino 1997: 50ff.; Chandler 1997: 83ff.), the family enterprise has persisted – dynamic, specialised, innovative, flexible, and adaptive to a rapidly changing environment, firmly rooted in regional, often local, entrepreneurial communities, and present in world-wide markets.

This renewal of interest in the virtues of family firms has been accompanied by a growing volume of theoretical and empirical research; the relevance of such firms to the wealth of the nation is illustrated by a growing number of MBA courses in European business schools that address the various aspects of family business management (Corbetta 2001). Likewise, consultants are increasingly specialising in the field. Since 1988, the *Family Business Review* has published quarterly issues on almost every aspect of the topic, both from a theoretic and an empirical perspective. In 1984 and 1990, respectively, two groups were founded: the Family Firm Institute (FFI) in the USA, and the Family Business Network (FBN), as its European counterpart. The FBN holds an annual conference summarising the results of academic research in the field.

The overlap between the firms and the family has encouraged analytical contributions from various other academic disciplines, principally sociology, psychology, and other behavioural sciences (2001).

From the historian's standpoint, the issue of family business is anything but new. While the changes in the perception and status of the subject suggest a number of issues (which this book will try also to summarise, by means of a critical discussion of the literature) for those who evaluate the past, the study of family enterprises offers significant contributions to the understanding of both national and international economic systems.

First of all, the contribution of family business must be analysed in the long run, i.e., across the three industrial revolutions, examining to what extent a relatively high presence of family firms in a capitalist industrialised country is an advantage – or a disadvantage – for a country's economic system. A second relevant issue concerns the relationship between a firm's size and its ownership and organisational structure; this topic involves as well the controversy regarding the (assumed) direct relationship between poor market performance and family-based ownership and organisational structure.

A further relevant point concerns the similarities and differences among various models of family firms, as well as the evolution of the family-controlled company following the radical changes in technology and markets since the first industrial revolution. The different roles and outcomes of family business enterprises must be evaluated by considering the nature of the production process and the overall sector. That is to say, the investigator must discriminate between commercialisation, finance, and manufacturing, and, inside the latter, between scale and capital-intensive industries on the one hand and traditional businesses, as well as innovative specialised suppliers, on the other.

These issues will run through the entire discussion of this book, which is divided into three chapters. In the first, 'Family business:

nature and structure', the definitions of 'family business' used by economists will be discussed in an attempt to offer a flexible conceptualisation of the family firm, stressing also its persistence in modern economies.

The following chapter, 'Geographical, sectoral, and dimensional distribution of family firms', will analyse the variations in the incidence of family firms inside the most advanced industrialised countries, including also the case of recently developed areas like East Asia and Latin America. The distribution of family firms by industry and by size is clearly influenced not only by technological forces, but also by national cultural patterns, which will be taken into account. The chapter also analyses the determinants of family businesses' vitality through time. Institutional factors are taken into consideration. These are both formal and informal and are influenced by a country's dominant culture which may be favourable or hostile to family firms. The structure of financial markets is another essential element in understanding the enduring success of family enterprises, especially where alternative sources of finance (banks and, above all, stock exchanges) are considered. Likewise, the legislative framework as well as a government's economic policies toward the economy have enormous impact on family firms. This is especially true in the presence of networks of interest involving the policymakers and the most important entrepreneurial families – the intensity of such networks varying considerably in different national cases.

The last chapter, 'Family firms in the era of managerial enterprise', discusses the impact of the changes in technology and market structures characterising the second and third industrial revolutions on family firms, focusing especially on the different versions of the Chandlerian model of evolution of the large modern managerial corporation. In this section the problem of the introduction of managerial hierarchies into family-controlled enterprises will be examined, highlighting the different experiences in various national contexts. A persistent identity of ownership and control in modern industries inevitably raises a problem of corporate governance and efficient allocation of resources that will be discussed as well. In the same chapter, the persistence of family firms inside modern economic systems will be analysed in the light of the transaction cost theory, looking at family firms as intermediate organisational structures between bureaucracy and the market. In this perspective, family business can be seen as the optimal solution, even in scale-intensive industries, when the managerial enterprise faces high transaction and agency costs in a hostile environment. Conversely, the persistence of family business can have a negative outcome: the absence of a corporate governance system inhibits the potential for strategic, technological, and organisational innovation; and the problem of leadership succession is chronic. Finally, the extensive use of family-based business networks in the emerging economies of East Asia and Latin America, in both production and distribution, will be examined as a possible confirmation of the essential role played by family firms in sustaining the take-off and the first phase of industrialisation.

Given the relevance of family business in both a political and economic perspective, a large amount of data is now available on the diffusion and the relevance of family business in different economies throughout the world. However, it is difficult to assemble comparable data, given the diverging definitions of family business adopted, reflecting a single country's history and culture. In this volume I will not draw an up-to-date quantitative picture of the presence of the family business in the developed economies: the data will be only partially used to highlight single aspects of more general issues.

This book is not a defence of the family business as the best way possible to organise an economic activity, where the 'human' and the 'rational' are mixed in a protective environment and the individual can best develop his/her talents and aptitudes (Schumacher 1973). It is not necessary to stress the evidence showing that family firms are the scenes of labour exploitation, of paternalistic and conservative labour relations, and where the individual can be subject to abusive discipline and control that can seldom be found elsewhere. Family firms are sometimes the opposite of a creative and innovative environment: largely path dependent, they avoid innovation and change as well as growth exceeding the family's resources and management capacity. It is not easy to maintain that family firms are superior to other forms of economic organisation, for instance in capital-intensive or research-intensive industries, where large managerial public companies dominate (Casson 2000: 198, 216). Equally, it is impossible to maintain the overall inferiority and inefficiency of the family firm – especially where, for instance, specialised or artisanal products are considered, or when the economic activity takes place in a turbulent environment with scarce information or without the guarantees present in a market-oriented society that safeguards private property.

The aim of this book is simply to review, even if only partially, the growing and often disparate homogeneous research on family business. A further goal is to give an idea of the historical evolution of this particular form of business organisation, its contributions to the economic growth of single economies, the reasons for its decline and also for its persistence, and the different forms that it takes over time depending on various business cultures and institutional environments. The outcome of this review should help those who are, for different purposes and from different perspectives, interested in this subject to identify the action, the strategies, the contribution as well as the failure and decline of family firms. The analysis is presented within a particular, historically defined economic, social, political, and above all institutional context. It is not sufficient to consider the family firm as a subject of study in abstract terms, as recently suggested: 'The impact of [entrepreneurial] behaviour upon the performance of the enterprise is mediated by the institutional environment in which the firm operates. In some environments the family firm is favoured, and in others it is not. Changes in the environment across industries and countries, and over time, explain the varying fortunes of the family firm' (2000: 204). Whilst it is a useful exercise to evaluate the contribution of family firms to economic growth and welfare, it is also important to contextualise the experience of family firms. This will at least prevent us from thinking of family business as a form of productive organisation suitable only for small and medium-sized firms, and as the same 'at every time and in every place' (2000: 201), two mistakes quite common among both economists and historians.

1
Family business: nature and structure

Despite its relevance, a useful definition of the family firm is elusive. By contrast, the large, managerial enterprise shows very well-defined features. It first appeared in manufacturing in the United States between the 1870s and the 1890s and was stimulated by pervasive waves of technological innovation in transportation and production, which are usually labelled 'the second industrial revolution'. It spread into capital-intensive industries – mostly chemicals, electrical products, transportation systems, petroleum refining, primary metals, some branches of the food and beverages industry, cigarette making, and several others (Chandler and Hikino 1997). The dimensional growth and the complex activity linking production and distribution triggered an organisational revolution as well; the relatively simple structures employed during the first industrial revolution evolved into the much more sophisticated U- and M-forms of organisation. These management structures were crowded by salaried low, middle, and top managers, more and more autonomous from the property and from the founder's family, according to the growing specialisation of their roles. Alfred Chandler put it best:

Salaried managers' specialised knowledge and their firms' ability to generate the funds necessary for continued expansion meant that they soon controlled the destiny of the enterprises by which they were employed . . . In the large, multiunit enterprise . . . salaried middle managers, who have little or no share in its ownership, have come to be responsible for co-ordinating the flow of goods and supervising the operating units.

(Chandler 1980: 12–13)

Displaced from middle management, the owners soon also lost their role at the top of the firm. As the growth of the corporation demanded more investment and financial resources, the shift from personal, family capitalism to financial capitalism, where bankers and other financiers shared top management decisions, occurred (1980: 13). In the end, however, given the growing complexity of the activities undertaken by the new, modern enterprises, the managers themselves were ultimately responsible for resource allocation and the most relevant strategic decisions. Quoting Chandler again:

> No family or financial institution was large enough to staff the managerial hierarchies required to administer modern multiunit enterprises. Because the salaried managers developed specialised knowledge and because their enterprises were able to generate the funds necessary for expansion, *they ultimately took over the top-level decision making from the owners or financiers or their representatives* [who] rarely had the time, the information or the depth of experience to propose alternatives; they could veto proposals, but they could do little else . . . Family members, as a result, soon came to view their enterprise, as did other stockholders, from the point of view of renters; that is, *their interest in the enterprise was no longer in its management but rather in the income derived from its profits*. Firms in which representatives of the founding families or of financial interests no longer make top-level management decisions . . . can be labelled *managerial enterprises*.
>
> (1980: 13–14; emphasis added)

These changes in the ownership structure of the large corporations are documented in the well-known research presented at the beginning of the 1930s by Berle and Means (1932). They presented clear (if partially criticised – see Burch 1972: ch. 1) evidence of the growing separation between ownership and control, as well as of the fragmentation of stock ownership which determined the birth of the so-called 'public company'. The radical transformation brought about by this new actor in social and political life does not need to be emphasised. Neither does its impact on the intimate structure of nations, and the revolution that occurred in the field of economic science subsequent to the emergence of oligopolistic and multinational corporations (see Galbraith 1967).

With the rise of the managerial corporation, the transformation of the industrial enterprise spread all over the world, bringing about a revolution in nations' competitive advantage (in a few decades the USA and Germany surpassed the world leader, Great Britain, in both GNP and international trading) (Elbaum and Lazonick 1986:9ff.). It also triggered the birth of some *first movers* able to establish enduring success in their fields and to gain long-standing leadership in national and international markets (Chandler 1990a). In this way, the modern business enterprise can be defined as 'an economic institution that owns and operates a multiunit system and that relies on a multilevel managerial hierarchy to administer it' (Daems 1980: 203–4). Implicitly, this kind of organisation cannot be owned and controlled by a family (Dobkin Hall 1988). Much more relevant is the fact that 'when this definition is accepted, the study of the modern firm becomes a study of when, where, and why business hierarchies were established to manage functional and vertical integration, with a resulting increase in aggregate concentration of assets' (Daems 1980: 204).

In search of a definition: quality and quantity

Contrary to the relatively easy definition of big business and of the modern managerial corporation, it is not as simple to delineate the boundaries and features of the family business, even from a 'residual' perspective. To begin with, the family firm is a form of productive organisation whose origin is impossible to locate precisely in place or time. Family firms were in the absolute majority during the first industrial revolution, as well as in the pre-industrial period, going from the urban artisan's workshop to the famous Medici Bank, investigated by Raymond De Roover (De Roover 1963), to the sophisticated commercial and trading company of Andrea Barbarigo, 'Merchant of Venice', and the sibling partnerships common in the same period among the merchants of the Adriatic Sea Republic (Lane 1944a and 1944b). The family firm is now the backbone of a significant number of recently industrialised economies, and still a lively presence in the 'old industrialisers', as well as in a large number of sectors, from the labour-intensive and craft-based to specialised suppliers.

The presence of the family firm inside a certain economic system is largely – if not completely – due to asymmetric information, a turbulent environment, and a legal system unable to secure and enforce property rights. Today, at least in advanced Western economies, the firm operates in a much less hostile environment than in the past (Cassis 1997: 123; Casson 2000: 205). However, the 'classic' family firm – in which property and control are firmly entwined, where family members are involved in both strategic and day by day decision-making, and the firm is shaped by a dynastic motive – is still a reality in almost all of the advanced economies, even those, such as the USA, that have been called the 'seedbed of managerial capitalism'.

From the perspective of managerial capitalism, it is theoretically possible to suggest a definition of the family firm based upon its size, whatever its measure. In this manner, the family firm should be considered as only one of the initial stages in the life of the enterprise, following the start-up period and preceding the public company phase (for a synthesis, see Dyer 1986: 4–5). Family firms in this model are generally small and medium-sized; slow growing; characterised by 'flat' organisational structures and internal succession patterns; relying upon self-financing or on local, often informal credit sources and avoiding stock-market finance; implicitly backward from the perspectives of production technology and labour relations; and less profitable than managerial ones. This is the usual perspective suggested by traditional economics (for a summary, see Casson 2000: 205–6). A considerable amount of evidence demonstrates, however, that, on the contrary, it is possible to find many examples of dynamic, large, and profitable family firms. In these examples, the traditional characteristics of proprietary capitalism – paternalism, dynastic motives, internal succession patterns, high dependence on local production systems – successfully mix with relatively 'modern' features of capital markets – internationalisation, technology utilisation, and so on. This is, for instance, the case with a large number of medium-sized and relatively large Italian family firms, well-known corporations in traditional as well as specialised industries such as Benetton, Luxottica, Ferrero, Natuzzi. They are active world-wide and rely on international financial institutions attracted to their high profit ratio. Incidentally, this had also been the experience of a number of *first movers* in almost all the European countries during the first half of the twentieth century, when the second industrial revolution spread all over the continent (see Dritsas and Gourvish 1997 and Cassis 1997). In his contribution to

Managerial Hierarchies, Leslie Hannah points out that it is very difficult to demonstrate that British family firms, also in capital-intensive industries, were less efficient than managerial ones, stressing the need for a less deterministic perspective in evaluating the relationship between the ownership structure and the general performance of the enterprise (Hannah 1980: 52ff.). While exploring the issue of organisational innovation, Terry Gourvish points out that the conservatism of British entrepreneurship before the 1960s is only partially connected to family persistence. Equally significant was a more general 'clubby, gentlemanly approach to such elements as management recruitment, staff development, and the application of organisational science to business' (Gourvish 1988: 41). In the well-known case of the glassmaking firm of Pilkington, for instance – cited by Alfred Chandler in *Scale and Scope* as a powerful example of the 'familialism' characterising British business (Chandler 1990a: 592) – it is true that in 1945 the board considered positively the fact that Alastair Pilkington (who was the inventor of the floating process and thus a powerful resource for the company) was a 'Pilkington', even if his branch of the family had had no connections with that owning the firm for at least fifteen generations. At the same time, it should not be forgotten that, as stressed by Theo Barker, the process of managerialisation and the co-optation of non-shareholder directors had started at Pilkington's between the world wars (Barker 1977: 320ff.), and that in the same minutes quoted by Chandler, the board declared – even if in a very cautious tone – themselves ready to prepare for the future by accepting truly promising candidates (1977: 417–18).

It seems in the end somewhat hazardous to suggest an explicit and direct relationship between a firm's size and the right form of ownership.

Likewise, it is also wrong to assume that family firms are in general less profitable and consequently less efficient than those run by managers. There has been a long debate on profitability because the field research on the subject provides variable results, differing from time to time, from country to country, and according to the industry (for a discussion and a brief summary, Hannah 1982: 4–5). There is a growing amount of research trying to link business performance to ownership structure but, since it tends to concern well-defined sectors and/or countries in what is usually a relatively short span of time, it is almost impossible to find incontestable results. (For a general overview, see Neubauer and Lank 1998: 11–12. See also, among the others, Monsen *et al.* 1968 on US major corporations during the 1950s; Burch 1972: 105–6 for the 1960s; Sheehan 1967: 182ff.; Savage 1979: 76ff.; Jacquemin and De Ghellinck 1980 on France during the 1970s; on the UK, Holl 1975, and Leach and Leahy 1991; at a 'micro' level, for an example of industry comparative perspective, see Church 1982. A significant case history stressing the comparison between a family firm and a non-family firm is provided by Sluyterman 1997 on the Dutch liqueur-maker De Kuyper.)

A sectoral criterion does not function adequately, either. In fact, efficient family firms are found not only in the craft-based, traditional, and labour-intensive industries, but also in scale-intensive industries and especially in specialised, customer-oriented industries. This means that a clear-cut sectoral division is impossible, even if it is evident that research-intensive activities characterised by long-term investments are found in large corporations with institutionalised research and development, while technology-intensive family firms exist largely in well-defined market niches with a limited innovative activity. It is easy to maintain that technology and capital-intensity growth coincide with a decline in the role of family firms (Yasuoka 1984b: 306). Also in this case, however, it is not difficult to find examples of family firms committed to innovation and technological research with considerable capital intensity at the same level as managerial corporations (Cassis 1997: 131). The sectoral typology is crucial; in some cases – for instance, in finance and insurance – the family firm is still resilient and largely present (Rose 1995b: xvi and xxv). David Landes provides a telling example of the role of family dynasties when high-transaction cost sectors are concerned. The story of the Bleichröder House from the mid nineteenth until the second half of the twentieth century provides an interesting example of the rise and fall of a family firm caused by the weaknesses of the dynastic motive – as well as a powerful illustration of the relevance of kinship ties in the early phases of the life of the enterprise. Landes particularly shows this to be the case when a crucial asset for the activity is rapid and reliable information. The author himself is no supporter of personal capitalism and suggests that in such cases the advantages brought by the family in terms of long-term commitment, know-how, and the cultivation of trust exceed or at least equal the disadvantages (Landes 1975). The twentieth-century history of old industrialisers provides considerable evidence in this respect. For instance, in the case of France, Emmanuel Chadeau has demonstrated the enduring presence of family-owned and family-managed large firms in capital-intensive advanced industries from the first industrial revolution until the present (Chadeau 1993).

A point related to this issue concerns the so-called short-sightedness of the family firm. In this perspective – shared by several historians such as Payne (1984, particularly pp. 196–7), Landes (1949), Sargant Florence (1961), and others – the family firm proves historically to be conservative in its policies of development and investment and, subsequently, unable to sustain growth and innovation, especially in capital and technology intensive industries. This is particularly the case when large size is concerned (for a review see Church 1993: 20–4; for a general critique of this perspective based upon historical evidence see Rose 1995b: xiv and xxi). At the micro level, the lack of commitment on the part of family firms toward innovation, combined with their short time horizons, is often associated with the decline of their dominance in capital-intensive industries. At the macro level, the same phenomenon is considered among the main weaknesses of a national economic system. In this respect Italy provides an interesting example of family firms' inability to cope with the new technological and productive challenges after the Second World War. During the economic boom of the 1950s and 1960s, some of the *first movers* in the capital-intensive industries of the second and third industrial revolutions – firms such as Lancia in the car industry, Olivetti in electronics, and several producers of household appliances, for example Ignis and Zanussi – lost their leadership position and undermined the future performance of the entire national economy (Pavan 1973; Amatori 1997a: 270ff.).

Notwithstanding these examples, it is clearly wrong, especially in a historical perspective, to draw conclusions about the inadequacy of the family business in sustaining the evolution of an industrial economy, both during the initial stages of development and also after (Brockstedt 1984: 261–2; Barker and Lévy-Leboyer 1982: 24; Cassis 1997). On the contrary, some authors, on the basis of empirical research, conclude that family-run companies are not only more profitable but also generally much more profit-oriented than managerial ones. Further, the inevitability of rapacious appropriation of dividends by a 'hungry' family is far from having been demonstrated (Donnelley 1964: 95; Yasuoka 1984a: 5; Monsen 1996: 26, 28). Likewise, 'short-termism' has been considered a negative feature among large conglomerates, resulting in the mergers and acquisitions wave of the sixties (Chandler 1994: 6; Rose 1995b: xvii). In the Italian example, again, a number of well-managed family firms were able to face the turbulent years of the economic boom and the following crisis of the 1970s (these were located in the already-mentioned household appliances industry and in the food and beverages and mechanical sectors). Meanwhile, during the same period, managerial, often state-owned corporations in technology-intensive industries – ENI in energy and chemicals, Montecatini and Edison in chemicals and electricity – were dramatically unsuccessful.

Another perspective often used in defining family business and implicitly related to the 'stages theory' is that of endurance and continuity. Implicitly, family business is considered, on average, to be not very long-lasting. Relatively quickly, in two or three generations, the entrepreneurial and family firm is supposed to evolve into a managerial, public company or to disappear, given the difficulties for the single family in managing a growing and complex activity. The so-called 'Buddenbrooks effect' (the third-generation dearth of entrepreneurial skills resulting in the decline of the firm) has been extensively investigated, and the resulting evidence challenges the 'three-generations paradigm' (start-up and early growth, consolidation, and decline – for an analysis of the stages, see Dyer 1986: 4–5) previously considered as distinctive of family firms (Barker and Lévy-Leboyer 1982: 10ff.; Rose 1993; Jones and Rose 1993: 5ff.). The recent study by Professor Hidemasa Morikawa (2001) is an impressively well-documented attempt to demonstrate the inescapable destiny of the family firm, i.e. the alternatives of managerialisation or decay. In a chapter which examines 'family enterprise in Japan today', he provides an impressive list of entrepreneurial failures due to the refusal to go public, to familialism and family feuding and to failed leadership succession. As Morikawa concludes:

My persisting view is that future prospects for family enterprises are not optimistic. The first reason for my rather pessimistic outlook is that successful family enterprises . . . are the exception rather than the rule. Also, even successful family enterprises find it difficult to have continued success over long periods of time owing to the problem of continually finding and training new and capable top managers from within the family. The same problem exists to an even greater degree with less successful family enterprises. These two issues . . . strengthen the argument that family enterprises are intrinsically limited in their future prospects.

(2001: 179)

Even if it is true that family firms evolve generally into managerial structures, it is not demonstrated that this is the only alternative to the decline and consequent 'death' of the company. The problem in perpetuating the active presence of the family at the head of the firm is without doubt the issue of succession. As is well known, problems of leadership succession arise where the family is not able to produce adequate leaders to take over the entrepreneurial role or, on the contrary, where too many of them are involved in the day-to-day management of the company. A typical and emblematic 'Buddenbrooks effect' case study, embedded in a contrast between different corporate cultures and problems of leadership succession, is that of the Austrian forwarding house Schenker, known worldwide (Stiefel 1997). The 'third-generation effect', moreover, continues to inspire novels and case studies – an excellent example is Levine's fascinating account of the decay of the House of Barneys department store chain (Levine 1959). In these cases the family ownership structure proves, according to its critics, to be weak and inefficient, and the consequence is stagnation and decline (in general, see Barker and Lévy-Leboyer 1982; for evidence see Savage 1979: 10ff.; a well-known, qualitative perspective on English experience is provided by Wiener 1981; this is also discussed in Rubinstein 1993; the evidence provided by single-company histories is enormous).

According to very recent research, the leadership succession pattern and its effect on the firm's survival is linked to such a high number of cultural, institutional, legal, and environmental factors that care must be taken to avoid dangerous generalisations. In a well-known section of his *Strategy and Structure*, Alfred Chandler, drawing on the Du Pont case, agrees that family firms succeed in maintaining their leadership positions when transition is carefully managed.

Despite the fact that members of the Du Pont family represent a substantial ownership interest in the company and are present in its management and policy making, family relationship, quite obviously, has not been the sole reason for promotion. This restraint on family prerogative, however, stems from Pierre Du Pont's deliberate rejection, in 1910, of the 'long entrenched, inherited attitude that the firm was managed for the family and the family was to manage the firm . . . Pierre did appoint family members to senior posts, but only after they had proven themselves managerially competent' (Chandler 1962: 64).

In some cases, adequately planned succession and training of new generations has proved to be an indispensable asset for the firm's expansion and prosperity. This is consistent with Mark Casson's suggestions about the counter-cyclical behaviour of family firms – slow to innovate in favourable periods, but benefiting from their 'cautious strategy' in times of crisis (Casson 2000: 202).

The chapter has so far presented only a few examples of the difficulty in defining, from a qualitative perspective, exactly what a family firm is (Ward and Aronoff 1996: 2). The task is not made any easier when looking at what are supposed to be more 'precise' parameters, such as ownership and control, stock capital property, number of seats on the board of directors, and so on. Using a quantitative perspective is also problematic. The degree of diffusion of family business in an economic system during a given period largely depends on the definition of the family firm that is adopted. For instance, according to recent research, at the turn of the twentieth century family firms were numerically consistent in most European industrialised countries. In Italy it was from 75% to 95% of all registered companies, in Spain 70%–80%, in the UK 75%, in Sweden more than 90%, in Switzerland 85%, in the Low Countries 80%–90%, and in Germany 80% (Neubauer and Lank 1998: 10; Colli, Perez, and Rose 2000). Similar data obtained from research on the European small and medium-sized enterprises at the beginning of the 1990s – defining family firms as the enterprises with a family shareholding exceeding 60% of the issued capital – found that on average two-thirds of the firms of the sample were family firms (Donckels and Frohlich 1991).

When big business is considered, the data available show a similar situation. At the end of the twentieth century 17% of the top 100 corporations, both in the USA and in Germany, were family firms, accounting for 8% and 12% of GNP respectively. Research published in 1993 demonstrated that among the top 5,000 major Dutch corporations, 46% were family-run companies (quoted in Sluyterman 1997: 106), while in the same period about one-third of the top 100 Swiss corporations were entrepreneurial or family firms (Müller 1996: 19). In Italy, the large family firm has been a permanent feature in the historical evolution of the country's industrial structure (Bairati 1988; Amatori and Colli 2000). In Italy at the beginning of the 1980s, 36% of the top corporations (about 170 in the Mediobanca's ranking), 13% of the capital, 12% of the total sales, and 15% of employees in the country were family-controlled (Gennaro 1985). According to some observers, even if the main corporations were modernising their ownership and organisational structure, the relevance of family shareholding was still considerable and far from declining (Chiesi 1986: 434). In any case, nearly 50% of the top 100 Italian corporations today are family-controlled; a much more comprehensive sample confirms the diffusion of family ownership at every level, sector, and dimension (Barca *et al*. 1994: ch. 1; Corbetta 1995: 3ff.). In 1980, family firms held the absolute majority of assets in the Japanese economy (Yasuoka 1984a: 3), while at the end of the same decade 95% of US companies were family-owned, and there is no evidence of a decline in this figure recently, particularly where traditional sectors are considered (Dyer 1986: ix).

These figures need to be carefully qualified. Variations in the definition of 'family business' can bring considerably different results. One interesting case is that presented in research published in 1972 by Philip Burch (Burch 1972). From the author's perspective, Berle and Means's findings on the emergence of the big corporation and the separation of ownership from control are fascinating and provocative; they are, however, misleading as they are based upon a too-restrictive definition of family business. Private ownership is described as holding more than 80% of the voting stocks; majority ownership is more than 50%; minority ownership is from 20% to 50%. In this way, the two authors neglect to consider a significant entity: the family firm in American industrial capitalism during the twentieth century. According to Burch, the persistence of family management and control among the top US corporations was still pervasive well into the twentieth century when a looser definition – 4%–5% minimum capital in the hands of an individual, a family, or a group of families, *and* inside *or* outside presence of one or more family members on the board of directors – had been adopted. In 1965, among the first 300 *Fortune*-ranked, publicly owned industrial concerns, only about 41% were under managerial control, nearly 43% were *probably* family-controlled, and the remaining were *possibly* under family control (Burch 1972: ch. 5, and p. 68 for the data). Figures provided for the 1950s on the 175 largest US corporations suggested that over 50% of them had 'close relatives or in-laws holding management jobs' in the same company (Donnelley 1964: 96). Adopting the same measure of ownership used by Berle and Means, by 1963, of the top 200 US corporations, more than 80% were under managerial control, only about 3% were labelled as 'majority ownership', and *none* could be considered under private ownership (Larner 1966). Another interesting inquiry into *Fortune*'s top-ranked corporations, published at the end of the sixties (Sheehan 1967) noted that under a 'conservative' definition of control – ownership of at least 10% of the voting stock by a single owner or by a family – about 150 out of the top 500 US corporations could be considered as family firms, concluding that 'the demise of the traditional American proprietor has been slightly exaggerated and that the much-advertised triumph of the organisation is far from total' (1967: 179). Again according to Larner (1970), at the beginning of the 1970s – the apex of the so-called 'American Century' – more than one-quarter of the top 300 US corporations were under family control. A recent report on family firms in the US economy (Shanker and Astrachan 1996) highlights this point. The authors provide an interesting taxonomy of mostly reliable statistics relative to US family firms, stressing the high variability of the results, not only with regard to the source considered, but also where different definitions of 'family firm' are taken into account. The definition of family firms is in fact highly subjective and far from being standardised (1996: 110–11). For instance, in the above mentioned report the estimated number of family firms present in the US industrial system varies from more than 20 million (more than 90% of the total of the firms) if a 'broad' definition ('some degree of family control') is adopted, all the way down to 4 million if a much more restrictive definition (multiple generations involved; direct family involvement in strategic decisions; 'more than one family member having managerial responsibilities') (109–10) is employed. There is also a considerable difference in GNP contribution (49% against 12%) and employment (59% of the workforce against 15%). Yet it is largely accepted as a matter of experience that, where a relatively large size requires some degree of separation between ownership and control, compelling the owner family to float a part of the stock capital, the 'proprietor' can maintain a *de facto* control over the enterprise with a small minority shareholding. This is so especially where this arrangement is accompanied by other devices which 'multiply' the voting power (for instance, the issuing of shares with reduced voting rights) or grant stability to the board members (shareholders' agreements). This is very common, as the following sections will describe in much more detail, in some countries where financial holdings and groups are largely dominant – thanks usually to favourable legislative frameworks – replacing the mechanisms of vertical integration. In Italy, for instance, but also in France and Belgium, historically the major privately owned corporations have been able, during the second industrial revolution and up to the present, to raise capital on the stock market while leaving – thanks to financial holdings, family trusts, pyramidal financial groups – the power of control in the hands of individuals or families. (On Italy, see for instance Amatori 1997b, and Bianchi, Bianco, and Enriques 2001; on France, in a historical perspective, Lévy-Leboyer 1984: 214ff., Chadeau 1993: 187, and more recently Fridenson 1997, who, however, emphasises the pattern of convergence of French big business toward managerialisation after the Second World War; and Schröter 1997: 187ff.; on Great Britain, see Kirby 1994.) In the case of the USA, well into the twentieth century, family control was possible thanks to similar financial 'tricks'. For example, at the end of the 1960s only about 10% of the outstanding shares of the Ford Motor Company were in the hands of the founder's nephews. But they were Class B shares (i.e., with a voting power of 3,492 votes per share), which granted the Fords control of 39% of the company. In the case of Du Pont, the family controlled 30% of Christiana Securities Ltd, which itself was entitled to 29% of the chemical corporation's shares (Sheehan 1967: 181). A large number of examples can be provided in this respect. Today some of the most important Italian industrial corporations, including Fiat and Pirelli, are family-controlled thanks to pyramidal arrangements and to shareholders' agreements, and nobody would deny the intense relationship existing between the Agnelli family and the strategic management of the whole group.

It is possible to conclude that in both the qualitative and the quantitative perspective it is difficult to give a complete and accurate definition of what exactly a family business is. We are in the presence of the classic 'concept too many', i.e., one so wide as to be necessarily inaccurate, especially in a statistical context. Whatever the definition given of 'family business', it is at best subjective, or has to be related to a defined context or period. It is possible to make an almost infinite taxonomy of suitable definitions (for example, see Neubauer and Lank 1998: 21–2). Today 'common sense' identifies the family firm with a small, labour-intensive unit at the initial stage of development, while a large number of family-run big businesses are to be found also in old industrialisers. Economists usually employ definitions capturing the essence of the phenomenon, implicitly referring to common sense and to well-defined contexts: for instance, the differences in the economic, legal, and institutional frameworks among, say, Italy, Korea, the USA, and Brazil will produce a different definition of family business (very similar considerations are in Rose 1994: 62). To define a family firm in the USA as one controlled with less than 5% of the voting capital is really too 'loose' a definition, while, thanks to the peculiar legal environment in Italy, the same quota there can be considered perfectly sufficient to exert control over the firm. The structure of the board of directors is also relevant, since, in the English case, even if often coincident, the inside director's role is legally and formally separated from that of the outside director. In several other European countries – with the notable exception of the German two-tier system – this distinction is not valid, and the same board covers jointly both the outside and inside functions. Given these limitations, in a historical perspective it is probably better to rely upon a loose definition of the family firm, flexible enough to cover all the possible situations while also encompassing the changing nature of the family itself, according to the period and geographical area considered.

The family (and the cultural and hence legal concept of 'family') is quite variable too. The European extended families of the early industrial period were in fact more similar in their economic behaviour to their counterparts today in Asia, India, the Far East or Africa, or to the Italian subcontracting family firm of the industrial districts, than to the present modern nuclear Western family. Jürgen Kocka emphasises, in his studies on the rise of the modern German corporation, the role of both family and bureaucratic culture in shaping the structure of the giant corporations (Kocka 1971, esp. pp. 136ff.). Hence, there are diverse structures to the family firm, and the need for different definitions. Very broadly, a family firm presents jointly the three elements of: kin (as defined accordingly within a particular cultural framework), property (the ownership of a significant fraction of the enterprise's capital), and control (authority over the strategic management of the company).

Mark Casson suggests splitting the definition into two parts – family-owned and family-controlled firms. This means that:

a firm is said to be family owned when family members own sufficient voting shares, or occupy sufficient places on the board of directors, to determine the appointment of the general manager or chief executive. A firm is said to be family controlled when the general manager is a member of this family. The definition of family ownership implies that the ownership of a significant minority stake by a single family does not necessarily qualify a firm to be a family firm . . . the stake . . . must be large enough to block any rival coalition of shareholders. The definition of family control refers to family members occupying key positions in management.

(Casson 2000: 199)

In this book a similar definition of family business is used since the key issue is not only ownership but above all that of control. The power to appoint the chief executive and possibly other components of the board coincides with the opportunity to manage the firm according to a family's values and culture. From another perspective, it allows the family to rely upon its own resources – in terms of reputation, knowledge, reduction of uncertainty, and low transaction costs – to run the business. It is a sufficiently broad and appropriate notion to describe a non-homogeneous concept like that of 'family business'.

The difficulties in finding a viable definition of 'family business' and the vagueness of the idea itself – variable according to place and time – raises another relevant question, particularly intriguing for the historian. As described at the beginning of this chapter, the transition from family firm to professional management has often been taken for granted, in the sense that it is technologically driven by the imperatives of scale and scope economies. This created the belief that, in general, family businesses are scarcely adequate to contribute to industrial growth in the capital- and research-intensive industries of the second and third industrial revolutions. In this way of thinking, the family business was considered as a legacy from a period where labour intensity, poor communications, and markets were of large but generally regional dimensions. In this way, family business was implicitly considered as appropriate for traditional labour-intensive industries but unsuitable for scale-intensive ones. According to this perspective, the convergence paradigm toward the model of managerial capitalism was in some senses unavoidable and, above all, almost self-imposing (Rose 1995b: xv). On the contrary, however, the history of family business demonstrates that the transition to the model of managerial capitalism has been generally slow and variable according to place and time. Meanwhile, in the big, capital-intensive corporations typical of the second and third industrial revolutions, families and dynasties have continued to play a significant role (Gourvish 1988: 34; Cassis 1997: 123). As Leslie Hannah has stressed:

Family majority shareholdings (and quite small minority interests, which, in a corporation with otherwise widely-depressed shareholding, may be sufficient for voting control) have been found to survive more widely than some early investigators suggested. In Europe, even more clearly, while there is an unmistakable degree of managerial control, the power of owners remains strong. It is evident that the 'Managerial Revolution' is a misnomer – at the very least the process is one of evolutionary change, and it proceeds at relatively slow pace.

(Hannah 1982: 2)

The persistence of the family firm as an economic actor – not only in the early phases of industrialisation and in small and medium-sized enterprises, but also in fields usually dominated by big managerial corporations – demonstrates that this institution maintains a considerable role and relevance in modern advanced economies. It is worthy of much more attention than has been given to it in the past (Rose 1995b: xiii–xiv).

Even if the presence of managerial hierarchies has often been implicitly seen as an alternative to that of family ownership and control, there is plenty of evidence that entrepreneurial dominance inside the firm is not necessarily exclusive. On the contrary, as Harold Livesay has stressed, looking at the US case:

> Bureaucracy...has not inevitably obliterated the entrepreneurial spirit necessary to the maintenance of capitalistic business systems. In the hands of the right protagonists it has become an instrument to cope with the complexities of doing business in the modern world. Bureaucracy, then, has not inevitably proven the nemesis of the entrepreneur; it has rather become a necessary tool of his trade. The success of men like Carnegie, Stoddard, and Ford [II, the founder's grandson], and the failure of so many others, demonstrates that the survival of the entrepreneurial spirit occurs because of bureaucracy, not in spite of it.
>
> (Livesay 1977: 443)

Changing perspectives on family firms

The evolution of studies dealing with family business mirrors the growing dissatisfaction with the traditional perspective on the effectiveness of the institution in modern economies (Rose 1995b: xiii). Before the 1970s, in fact, the family firm was scarcely considered by social scientists and, when it was, the focus was generally on issues other than family firms' proper nature and structure. In fact, both the research on the transformation in the financial and ownership structure of big business, and the 'technocratic' approach – stressing the necessary separation of ownership and control – view the family firm as a 'step' toward more advanced organisational structures (see, for instance, Chandler 1962, Marris 1964 and Galbraith 1967). From the perspective of business history, both the 'robber barons' literature and the much more advanced research of the Center for Entrepreneurial History at Harvard, even while offering an impressive bulk of case studies on family firms, rarely went beyond the analysis of individuals, and did not take into account the issue of the family firm *per se*.

During the 1960s and 1970s a considerable body of literature and research on family firms was published by academics and consultants. Organisational scientists in particular produced some work on the strategy and structure of family firms, trying to analyse their strengths and weaknesses under a more systematic perspective, even if adopting a simple and schematic approach (Corbetta 2001). From this standpoint, the coincidence of property and control, especially when the corporate size was considerable, was assumed to be an obstacle to growth and competitive strength, particularly where the issue of succession was concerned (see, for instance, Levinson 1971; Barry 1975; Barnes and Hershon 1976; McGivern 1978).

A change took place at the beginning of the 1980s and continued into the 1990s. The process of restructuring undertaken by major corporations, the 'de-merger' movement, and the crisis and decline, especially in Europe, of state-owned enterprises, together with the unquestionable success of a 'familialistic' Japanese model, provoked a reconsideration of the structure and dynamics of family firms. The model could be perceived now as providing a potential advantage in periods characterised by uncertainty and market failures. In some cases, this development was almost ideological in the sense that the decline of the American multinational was perceived as the symbol of the defeat of capitalism. The family firm, however, presented a human dimension where 'people mattered'. It also held out the prospect of a new production model – one much more creative and less impersonal, moulded by elements like friendship and kinship.

From a less impressionistic point of view, the continuing presence of family firms in almost all the advanced economies was validated by the existence of efficient alternative forms of productive organisation. These were based upon networks and groups of enterprises which had spread all over the industrialised world, from the Japanese *keiretsu* to the clusters of small enterprises in the industrial districts of Italy. These well-established developments presented undeniable evidence of an enduring legacy. The transaction cost theory became a very powerful instrument with which to emphasise the positive nature and role of family firms in modern economies. (See the seminal article of Ben-Porath 1980 and Pollak 1985: 585ff., 591.) This was especially true in sectors such as insurance and financial services where 'moral hazard' was particularly relevant, or where agency costs were relatively high (Pollak 1985: 591). Naomi Lamoreaux tested this point in her research on New England, where, from the beginning of the industrialisation process in the early nineteenth century, personal connections and family networks in banking played a crucial role in providing financial resources for early manufacturing enterprise (Lamoreaux 1994: 24ff.).

In a theoretical context, the new institutionalism provides a convincing explanation of alternative forms of economic organisation within the two extremes of markets and hierarchies (Granovetter 1996; Hamilton and Feenstra 1996). It is particularly useful in the study of those economies – such as the new industrialisers of the Far East – where big business is consistent with family-based organisational forms (Hamilton 1996; Fruin 1998). On the basis of transaction cost theory, however, it has been possible to build another conceptual framework relevant to the analysis of the family firm in a historical and comparative perspective. Evolutionary theory (for a general description, see Nelson 1994) stresses the diversity in organisational forms created by historically determined routines which in turn affect the choice of technology. From this perspective, the prevalence of a particular business institution is the result of a set of choices concerning technology and organisation taken over time and in a particular cultural context (Langlois and Robertson 1995: 150).

It is the combination of evolutionary theory, transaction cost theory, and the analysis of trust-based institutions and networks that provides an important conceptual framework to explain the family firm's persistence in the era of big business (Casson 1993: 43; Casson 2000: 215–16; Rose 1999).

From the 1980s onwards new research has considered the way the family firm has contributed to general economic development in a positive light. On the micro side, the main themes have been the relationship between strategies and structures of firms and family ownership, the introduction of professional managers, and the succession process. In a macro perspective, the research has examined the contribution of family firms to the wealth of the nation and the relationship between the diffusion of family firms, their persistence and the cultural and institutional environment.

Economic historians have contributed to this debate from the very beginning. Their work has provided a considerable amount of single-case research – providing company histories focusing both on succession and on leadership transmission strategies. It has also analysed the evolution of the institutional environment that shaped the different strategies and behaviour of the economic actors involved. As a consequence, the new institutionalism in its 'macro' perspective provides useful analytical tools. The complex system of formal and informal rules in which decisions are undertaken is relevant, while history is vital in explaining its evolution (North 1990). Especially relevant is the institutional context where family firms are concerned:

> Since the institutional environment is clearly influenced by historical forces it has especial relevance for the study of the behaviour of all firms, and in this context of family firms, in an international or even an intra-national perspective. The development of laws are path-dependent, so that there can be, for example, significant international differences in both the privilege and restrictions faced by family businesses. The legal status and degree of regulation of particular types of company-form, or the level of tariff protection enjoyed, may therefore vary between countries. As a result, even where ownership and control are united, family firms in different environments may display varying characteristics, capabilities and degree of longevity.
>
> (Colli and Rose 1999: 28)

In other words, the presence and persistence of family firms is not to be seen *solely* as the result of a particular set of technological, financial, legal, and market conditions, but also as able to influence the political context and hence the legal system and framework in which they operate. This is for instance true where *business elites* are concerned.

> (Cassis 1994: 243–4; Cassis 1997: 225ff.)

The discussion of the role of family firms in modern industrial development increasingly emphasises the extent to which the organisational structure adopted by an enterprise is the result of a complex array of forces rather than simply being related to technological issues. The relationship between the evolution of production technologies, capital intensity, and organisational structure is not therefore perceived mechanically, while considerable emphasis is given to the impact of institutional variety. In this context, efficiency becomes the result of a compromise in which culture and history play a significant role.

As a result, research on family firms has recently highlighted the connection between national cultural values and the diffusion of the family firm as a privileged way of organising economic activity well beyond the initial stages of the industrialisation process. This connection can be fully understood only through historical analysis. The diffusion of family ownership and control at any level in the countries of continental Europe, from France to Italy and even to small highly internationalised economies like the Dutch, Belgian or Swiss (Schröter 1997; Whittington and Mayer 2000: 87ff.), is a product of a kind of capitalist culture emphasising continuity, long-term perspective, and collusive behaviour. The persistence of this culture is clearly crucial for the long-lasting success of the so-called 'Rheinisch capitalism.' It also explains the difficulties in the way of, and the resistance to the transition toward, a 'third way' between the Anglo-American and continental models of capitalism (Albert 1991; Cassis 1997: 71; Dore 2000).

In conclusion, what has emerged in recent years is a growing awareness of the need both to move beyond the dichotomy between family and managerial firms, and to abandon the determinism of convergence. Current research on family firms has become multi-disciplinary, drawing upon sociology, politics, and management just as much as on economics and history. There has been a growing tendency to analyse the role of family firms at the different stages of growth of a defined national economic system. Significant case-study evidence in Western economies now shows that family firms may have a positive influence in some sectors, especially in services, as compared with publicly owned and managerial companies in other spheres. The persistence of family firms in the capital-intensive industries of the second and third industrial revolutions should not be considered as the consequence of a supposed incapacity of European and Asian entrepreneurs to understand and adopt the managerial models of the American corporation. Instead, the enduring presence of a particular form of business organisation can be seen as the best demonstration of its 'efficiency' against a defined institutional framework, rather than as a failure.

2

Geographical, sectoral, and dimensional distribution of family firms

The world-wide diffusion of the family firm confirms the impression that its relevance is dependent upon a complex array of institutional forces, and it is not merely a device to handle uncertainty during the initial phases of industrialisation. However, it is clear that the degree of diffusion of the family firm depends largely on the stage of economic growth, on the sectors involved, and on the structure of the enterprise itself *inside* those sectors. As shown in the previous section, today family firms remain important in most advanced modern economies. They can be found not only in traditional, small-scale, and labour-intensive industries but also at the top of the national rankings of industrial enterprises by sales and size, even if in some countries this presence is more significant than in others. Nevertheless, there are international differences in family firms' pervasiveness and structure, even if their contribution to GNP converges. Recent research has shown that 42 of the top 100 corporations in Italy were family-owned, while 17 of the top 100 companies in the USA and in Germany were family firms. The sales average of these companies per year was 2.7 billion Euros in Italy, 12.5 in Germany, and about 40 in the USA. The average number of their employees was nearly 134,000 in the USA, 58,000 in Germany, and about 14,000 in Italy. Notwithstanding these differences, in all these countries the contribution of the top family firms to GNP is very similar – about 10% (Montemerlo 2001: 20). A closer look would probably reveal that the sectors to which the top family corporations belong are slightly different from country to country, as well as the degree of coincidence of property and control in the company, the role of the board of directors, the relationships with employees, and so on (Corbetta and Montemerlo

1999; Montemerlo 2001: 21ff.; Corbetta and Tomaselli 1996). All this confirms the impression that – as for big business – the 'form' of the family firm largely depends upon the national context and on the historical conditions that shaped its particular path of development. In other words, the idea of a cross-national and cross-sectoral similarity among family firms is probably an oversimplified approach (Colli and Rose 1999: 24). To be more precise:

> In establishing why family business has been proved more resilient and successful in some regions and sectors than others and why, despite some common characteristics, its form and capabilities may vary it is necessary to look beyond purely economic variables. The analysis of such issues as attitudes to the family, to inheritance and to the community are critical to any understanding of family firm reactions to risk, uncertainty and other economic stimuli in different societies. Equally they inform any discussion of the international differences in the strategy and structure of family business.
>
> (Rose 1995b: xviii)

Stages of the industrialisation process

The different degrees of diffusion and persistence of family business can be explained by several factors, all embedded in a particular set of social, cultural, and historical conditions. Firstly, the stage of industrialisation reached by the country considered is relevant since the family firm is likely to be particularly important during the initial phases of industrialisation: simple technology, small scale of production, uncertainty, risk, scarce information, and imperfect formal institutions (Ben-Porath 1980; Alvesson and Lindkvist 1993). As Alexander Gerschenkron and later Sidney Pollard pointed out (Gerschenkron 1962; Pollard 1981), the patterns of diffusion of the industrialisation process from Britain to continental Europe differed widely from country to country, depending on national conditions and the role of *substitutive factors*. The family firm, however, has been constant in sustaining the industrialisation process, as comparative research suggests (see, for instance, the essays by Kozo Yamamura on Japan, Peter L. Payne on Great Britain, Claude Fohlen on France and Jürgen Kocka on Germany published in the seventh volume of the *Cambridge Economic History of Europe* edited by Peter Mathias and Michael Postan in 1978). For instance, a comparison between Britain and a relatively late industrialiser like Italy confirms the key function of the family firm at the beginning of the industrialisation process as well as during the period between the two World Wars. In Britain from the late eighteenth century and in Italy from the 1880s, family and community-based networks developed in response to uncertainty and market failure. At least until 1945, the business structures of both countries were dominated by family capitalism. Proprietorships and small-scale, often networked family firms characterised the early stages of industrialisation, especially in the staple industries. Family partnerships appeared in Britain during the eighteenth and nineteenth centuries in most branches of manufacturing, commerce, and finance. They were also the norm in brewing, shipbuilding, glassmaking, chemicals, and provincial banking. Outside manufacturing, they were common in retailing. Unity of ownership and control was also a striking characteristic among the financial institutions of the City of London. The popularity of family-oriented enterprise in eighteenth- and nineteenth-century Britain was a product of a complex interaction of legal, economic, and cultural forces. With the spectre of bankruptcy ever present, a combination of the common-law partnership and unlimited liability meant that many businessmen preferred to be associated with their family and community-based connections rather than with outsiders. Mary Rose, for example, has analysed in detail the rise of a network economy in the Lancashire cotton industry during the eighteenth and nineteenth centuries. Her work has stressed the contribution of a dense web of personal and kinship connections – occasionally reinforced by intermarriage strategies – to the diffusion of information, innovation, credit and finance, and commercial intelligence (Rose 2000: ch. 3).

In the Italian case as well, the family firm was the predominant form of enterprise during the whole period preceding the country's industrial take-off before the end of the nineteenth century. In manufacturing and commerce family firms were often present, especially in staple and export goods. The best examples can be found in those industries linked to agriculture, i.e., the food industry, and, above all, the silk industry. The latter strictly linked manufacturing with the primary sector, and gave rise to a considerable number of family enterprises active both in raw silk export and in commerce. The financial resources derived from silk were at the origin of a wide number of family-run banking houses, usually founded by the silk merchants. Even if the worm-breeding was carried out by peasants and farmers, and the silk spinning and weaving was initially run by landowners and then by 'pure' entrepreneurs (merchant-entrepreneurs), the nature of the firm and management did not change. The silk business was in this way dominated by the family firm or by partnerships among families of merchants and entrepreneurs. The same can also be said of other basic industries such as metallurgy (dominated on a local basis by small family firms or partnerships – particularly in scale-intensive phases of the production process, for instance smelting and refining), mining, and the engineering industry. Cotton manufacturing, another key staple industry in the country's first industrial revolution, began in the first half of the nineteenth century as a typical proto-industrial activity. Merchant-entrepreneurs put out raw cotton to weavers and sold the finished products on the market. This organisational structure was rooted in family enterprises which proved able to manage the complexity of putting out local networks. By the end of the century the cotton industry had been transformed into a much more modern sector based upon industrial concentration. However, the internal structure of the industry continued to be based upon families' and relatives' partnerships (Colli and Rose 1999: 31ff.).

Other late comers such as Spain are very similar, with family firms playing an important role in the early phase of industrialisation in the staple industries (Pérez 1997 and 2000). In the Low Countries too, family firm networks were the backbone of one of the most important sectors of the Dutch economy, that of edible oils and margarine (Arnoldus 2002). In Greece, family networks were essential during the initial stage of industrialisation in granting protection, as well as financial resources, to the first entrepreneurs (Dritsas 1997). The German case has been investigated in detail by Jürgen Kocka and he emphasises the relevance of family-based organisational structures that solved the problems of labour supply, motivation, finance, trust, and know-how typical of the early stages of the industrialisation process (Kocka 1999: ch. 5).

The family as a device to reduce transaction costs, as a source of information, and a reservoir of skill and finance was therefore at the core of the industrialisation process. For instance, in the Swiss chemical industry, family firms formed an extended supportive and exclusive network (Müller 1996: 28; Schröter 1997: 187). The well-known case of the Japanese *zaibatsu* before the Second World War is also significant in this respect. Even if, according to some scholars, the separation of ownership from control and the 'managerialisation' of the Japanese enterprise system took place well before the Second World War (Miyamoto 1984; Morikawa 1992; Morikawa 1997: 310; Takeda 1999; Morikawa 2001), the Meiji period saw the establishment of a strict relationship between state industrialisation policies and the strategies of some wealthy families that were moving toward diversified enterprise groups (Yamamura 1978). The large, conglomerate family-run *zaibatsu* typical of the Japanese experience have been replicated in several cases of late industrialisation, especially in East Asia (Amsden and Hikino 1994). As Alice Amsden suggests in analysing the pattern of industrialisation of late-industrialising economies: 'The long-standing difficulty in "late-industrialising economies" of forming firms in which professionals (salaried employees) manage and co-ordinate complex, large scale operating units partially stemmed from the difficulties of juxtaposing salaried management with family ownership, the predominant form of business enterprise in "late-industrialising economies" as late as 2000' (Amsden 2001: 191–2). The South Korean case is interesting in this respect because industrial take-off began immediately in the early 1960s and was based, as in the Japanese case, upon family-controlled, diversified big business groups called *chaebol*. The only – but relevant – difference from Japan is that the state denied the *chaebol* their own banking affiliates and could in this way directly control credit allocation and consequently the whole economic system (Amsden 1997: 336). Despite the presence of salaried managers, until the beginning of the 1990s the coincidence of ownership and control remained unchallenged; the *chaebol* accounted at the end of the 1980s for nearly 43% of total manufacturing (Kang 1997: 46). The families maintained a strict control over the entire group thanks to a complex system of cross-shareholding and they could also count on state support, which from the beginning took the form of an active policy of protection from, and especially incentives to, foreign competition (Amsden 1997: 364). It is worth suggesting that family control over the *chaebol* and hence the existence of an 'industrial élite' has surely been central to state industrial policies, facilitating the 'bargaining' process (Koike 1993: 365). On the other hand, the Korean case is also an example of the risks in such an industrialisation model, namely the tendency of the private interest of the family to over-determine the rational management of the group (Amsden 2001: 192). A similar example is that of Indonesia and other less developed countries in the Pacific Rim (for this, see the essays on business groups in Thailand, Indonesia, Korea, Taiwan, and the Philippines in Koike 1993). In this setting, the industrialisation process was driven by family firms which were generally active at the beginning in textiles and trading and then diversified into other activities while maintaining their original character as family-controlled and family-managed concerns. Despite some significant differences and whatever the name (from the Japanese *zaibatsu* and the Korean *chaebol* to the Indonesian enterprise groups), the structure remains substantially the same, with an extended family controlling key management positions during the enterprise's phase of expansion (Wong 1985; see Chapter 3 of this volume for a further discussion of the role of family firms in the Asian economic growth).

In a completely different historical, social, and cultural perspective are the Latin American *grupos* – defined as 'a multi-company firm which transacts in different markets but which does so under common entrepreneurial and financial control' (Leff 1978: 663 (retd in Rose 1995a: 499); Lansberg and Perrow 1991). Originating in the 1920s–1930s and after, today they are a relevant form – probably today the most relevant form – of business enterprise in the region.

Industry typology

Another factor relevant in explaining the persistence of the family firm well beyond the early phases of the industrialisation process is the nature of the sector involved, together with the general legal framework in which the economic activity takes place. In other words, family firms tend to persist in those sectors in which transaction costs – even in the presence of advanced legal systems – are higher than in others because of the nature of the activity itself. For instance, historically the evolution of the British financial sector shows an enduring presence of family-owned and family-controlled merchant banks (Chapman 1984). Family control persisted in

English merchant banking after the Second World War and well into the 1980s, influencing the present status of the internationally powerful and sophisticated British financial system. In this case, the reasons for the persistence of family control are linked to the 'social characteristics of merchant banking dynasties' (on this see extensively Cassis 1994, especially 208ff.), which were particularly efficient (and, as a result, sustained by the Bank of England). In this form, based upon a 'personalised and confidential mode of capital raising and financial diplomacy', 'The "gentlemanly" organisation of merchant banking reduced the need for great competence or effort on the part of family directors . . . In the terms of the continuity of dynastic possession, the crucial outcome of gentlemanly organisation was widespread agreements about the limits to competition and the desirability of mutual aid as a strategy for collective survival' (Lisle-Williams 1984: 245). The case of overseas Chinese family firms in East Asia confirms this phenomenon in another completely different geographical, historical, and cultural context. In 1995, for example, 47 of the 50 largest overseas Chinese business groups were engaged predominantly in 'property development and banking and finance activities', where interpersonal contacts and networking are the main competitive advantages (Ampalavanar Brown 1995: 3ff.).

Also, when non-financial sectors are examined there are cases in which a peculiar typology of the production process seems to be consistent with family enterprises of impressive dimensions. A valuable piece of research was published in 1995 comparing management practices and business structures in Britain and France (Cassis, Crouzet, and Gourvish 1995). The authors devote an entire section to the analysis of successful family firms able to grow and modernise their organisational structures, while remaining ultimately owned and directed by the family. In the cases of the food companies of Rowntree and Cadbury in Britain, or the French hypermarket and supermarket chains (Leclerc, Carrefour, Promodès, and Casino), the family firm seems able to maintain an advantageous position over a long period. This happens as well in the case of Cristofle, a French silversmith that has been able to join an artisanal philosophy with global sales (Fitzgerald 1995; Chadeau 1995; De Ferrière 1995). At Carrefour, the French chain of hypermarkets founded at the end of the 1950s, the role of the two founding families, Defforey and Fournier, seems still to be relevant, both from the ownership perspective and also in the style of management (Lhermie 2001: 51ff.). From this perspective it is clear that a conscious strategy of differentiation – a key strategic resource in consumer goods, distribution, fashion, luxury goods, and so on – is perfectly consistent with the existence of family firms both small and large (Cassis 1995: 20).

This is not the place to discuss the relationship between markets, demand structure, and the scale of production, which has been carried on extensively elsewhere (see Piore and Sabel 1984; Verley 1997; Sabel and Zeitlin 1997). It is only necessary to suggest that, in analysing the persistence and resilience of the family firm, it is necessary to consider also the morphology of the final demand. For instance, in the case of a highly differentiated consumption market, the firm would rely much more on extensive networks of knowledge and stable, handed-down know-how, than on bureaucratic structures; this is perfectly consistent with the persistence of family firms in mass retailing in Europe. This is probably a much more satisfying explanation than the traditional 'neoclassic' interpretation, according to which the persistence of family firms in labour-intensive and commercial sectors is connected to their comparatively low degree of profitability, which, in turn, keeps away the venture capitalists in search of high remuneration.

Financial systems

Where manufacturing is concerned, it is clear that technology is not the only force shaping the form of the enterprise. Even where scale and scope economies lend a powerful impulse toward growth and subsequent managerialisation of enterprise, Chandler has demonstrated that the reaction of the entrepreneurs to the technological push of the second industrial revolution would be shaped by several factors. These include national culture, legal standards, and the institutional framework, one part of which is the financial and banking system.

The structure of the financial market is especially important in explaining the persistence of forms of personal capitalism in well-advanced economic systems. In the case of several European countries, for example, the banking system acted at the beginning as a powerful instrument of modernisation, acting as a substitute for spontaneous enterprise.

The Italian case highlights the role that a particular set of financial market arrangements plays in shaping the form of business. In Italy, after the 1930s, the failure of the 'universal-bank model' in the absence of well-developed stock markets brought the diffusion of family-controlled financial holding companies that headed the main industrial groups. As a consequence, in some cases – as in the French one before the 1980s, but above all the Italian case until now – big business had been dominated by pyramidal holdings and Chinese-boxes, enabling the main shareholders, usually also inside directors, to control the corporation with a very small direct investment of capital and a much reduced risk of hostile take-over. To give an idea of the relevance of this mechanism in explaining the persistence of family control, it is sufficient to cite that now, at the beginning of the new millennium, thanks to the mechanism of the group (defined by law as a set of companies with separate legal status but controlled, both directly and indirectly, by the same subject), the main shareholders of the biggest Italian industrial corporations could multiply by *eight* (on average) their own resources directly invested in the enterprise's capital (Bianchi, Bianco, and Enriques 2001; Bianco and Casavola 1996: 437).

The diffusion of the group form at any level has been identified as a typical feature of Italian capitalism (Barca *et al.* 1994: vol. II, ch. 4) and in a historical perspective this form was quite common in Italy from the beginning of the industrialisation process (Amatori 1997b). Italian big business at the beginning of the nineties was, as a consequence, labelled as 'oligarchic family capitalism' where 'the main controlling shareholders are still clearly coincident with a small number of families, some of ancient entrepreneurial tradition, like the Agnelli, Pirelli, Orlando and Falck families, and some others relatively new' (Brioschi, Buzzacchi, and Colombo 1990: 165).

Institutional framework

It is unnecessary to stress that in this process a strategic role is played by the legal and institutional system that defines the general framework in which entrepreneurial action takes place. The legal system, together with industrial policies, is sometimes the main factor in the persistence of a particular form of personal capitalism. In some cases the constraints put up by the legislative framework also help to explain the persistence of family firms over time. This is, for instance, the well-known case of the 'Bubble Act', which is considered to be one of the main determinants of the personal form of British capitalism (Wilson 1995: 44–5; Rose 1994: 64). On the continent, and in a successive stage of development, the necessity of continuity and stability presented family firms with the need to raise substantial resources for capital-intensive initiatives. This led, for instance, to the introduction of a particular legal form at the end of the nineteenth century, the *Gesellschaft mit beschränkter Haftung* (*GmbH*), i.e., limited liability (Kocka 1999: 127). It was a solution quickly adopted elsewhere in Europe, as in France and Italy after the Second World War (Hau 1995; Ungari 1974: 74).

Inheritance laws also play an active role in determining the prevalence and persistence of family firms in different countries. The presence of inheritance laws prescribing an equal subdivision among heirs, or, alternatively, the existence of primogeniture, is an important factor shaping the strategies of succession in the family firm, and hence its governance and performance. During the early phases of European industrialisation the necessity to ensure the continuity of the family firm while observing inheritance laws brought about different solutions. To avoid fragmentation of the enterprise, daughters almost never expected to take an active part in the firm's management and were therefore indemnified, especially under the form of marriage settlements. It is interesting to note that this liquidation was often left as a long-term credit in the firm's liabilities. Usually the authority of the first son, or of the chosen successor, went unchallenged: the other sons were expected to undertake minor roles – for instance a top position in one of the commercial branches of the enterprise – or, alternatively, to search for another job. Sometimes, at least in the case of independent professionals such as lawyers or consultants, the link with the family business would remain strong. Marriages between cousins were common among the industrial dynasties of the nineteenth and twentieth centuries; in this way it was possible to maintain control over the enterprise, thus avoiding its fragmentation (Hau 1995: 56–7).

Another strategy to preserve the unity of the enterprise was to create a joint-stock company that, thanks to voting syndicates and shareholders' agreements, gave the appointed successor unchallenged authority. From this perspective the widespread presence of the holding form in continental Europe (Jones and Rose 1993: 11; Schröter 1997: 187–8) can also be explained because it was the best instrument to manage the family's interests. The heirs' stocks were conferred to the holding, which granted the firm's continuity and management (Hau 1995: 54–5). In other cases, there was external pressure to promote the transformation of the legal status of the firm into that of a joint-stock company, as happened in Germany when the country's main banks, wishing to monitor their investments more closely, put heavy pressure on the owner families to change the legal shape of the firm, thus enabling the banks' directors to enter their *Vorstand* (Supervision Board) (Kocka 1999: 166ff.). It is necessary to note that this did not mean the creation of 'pure' public companies. As Kocka (167) puts it:

Not every AG was a manager-enterprise, if by manager-enterprise one means an enterprise in which decisions and authority are carried out by salaried managers rather than by owners. Very often, especially if an existing firm was restructured as a joint-stock company, the AG merely represented a legal form within which the founders or their family continued to hold the decisive vote and exercise control: a family business in AG clothing.

Neither was this so in the French case, where the degree of family control, even in heavy industries – for instance, in iron and steel – remained very high (Miller 1981: 75ff.). For example, in the prominent manufacturing region of Lorraine, the local iron and steel industry was dominated by a number of entrepreneurial dynasties that were linked together by a complex network of financial and kinship ties until well into the twentieth century. During the nineteenth century, the legal form of the enterprise evolved from family firm to family partnership. Then, given the capital requirements generated by the steady growth of production, the *commandite par actions* (limited share-partnership) spread as the most frequently adopted legal form of the enterprise. The share-partnership evolved as an intermediate form between the partnership *tout court* and the joint-stock company; it was not so 'closed', since the shares could be bought and sold, and this made access to financial capital easier. However, the identification between ownership and personal management was not challenged, as it was in the joint-stock companies, where the authority in the board was to be shared among various individuals. The *société anonyme* became common in the Lorraine iron industry during the last quarter of the nineteenth century thanks to the flow of new capital from outside the region. In any case, this did not mean the creation of public companies or the decline of family capitalism. Very often, the new joint-stock companies were no more than the transformation of existing share-partnerships; the families were able in this way to maintain strict control over the day-to-day management of the enterprise as well to obtain fresh financial resources (Moine 1989: 121ff.). Also, in the United States, 'early . . . business corporations were as much family businesses as were partnerships'; their origins are to be found in the collective action of interconnected families, which reinforced these links also by means of interlocking directorships (Rose 2000: ch. 3).

Given the scarcity of comparative historical research in this field (Colli, Perez, and Rose 2000), it is difficult to present clear evidence of the influence of inheritance laws on the strategies and structure of family firms in differing national contexts. This issue is undoubtedly relevant, especially when one considers that, in the British case again, a radical shift in the legal system, with a sharp rise in death duties at the beginning of the 1950s, has been one of the main forces in the transformation of British industrial capitalism.

On the other hand, it is very often a lack of regulation that helps to explain the sense and success of the family enterprise, as the best organisational form when uncertainty and risk are high. In his detailed research on the Alsatian dynasties of entrepreneurs, Michael Hau has demonstrated that the enduring logic of the family firm is strictly connected to the culture of independence and autonomy consistent with an area that has been historically distant from the administrative and bureaucratic centre (Hau 1995: 44).

The legislative framework is also relevant in another context. As suggested above, family firms are a powerful tool for economic policy intended to stimulate industrialisation and growth. Private interests are strictly connected with public needs, and in the first phases of the industrialisation process the intervention of the state is frequently intended to sustain private family business. In some cases, the interests of the state and those of the leading families are so intertwined that it is difficult to distinguish between them. In the case of the new industrialisers of East Asia, for example, the relationship between the private, diversified big family firms and the state is very close. Again, the case of South Korea is significant in this respect. As industrialisation got underway in the late twentieth century, the *chaebol* big family-controlled diversified concerns were strictly disciplined by the state to avoid concentration of power in the hands of a minority (Hamilton 1998: 188; Amsden 2001: 225). They are also, however, managed as a powerful instrument by the government to promote industrialisation and competition in foreign markets (Jones and Rose 1993: 4; Chen 1995: 162–3; Lee 1997, esp. 9–10). In the words of Alice Amsden, 'in Korea and Taiwan, subsidies have been allocated according to the principle of "reciprocity", in exchange for concrete performance standards that are monitored by fairly competent state officials' (Amsden 1997: 363). Significant in this respect is the case of the Salim Group, the largest corporation in Indonesia with over 150,000 employees. Founded immediately after the Second World War by Liem Sioe Liong, a Chinese immigrant, the firm expanded, thanks to personal contacts inside the local Chinese community and also to the close connections that the founder was able to establish with military forces to supply foodstuffs, clothing, medicines, and arms. The enterprise developed in the form of a diversified group with significant financial activities (e.g., Bank of Central Asia) during the sixties and after the nationalisation of Dutch companies in 1957. When Suharto came to power in 1965, the Liem Group began a steady growth thanks to an alliance with the military power, which took the form of real partnerships. Suharto's stepbrother, a son, and a daughter were among Liem's partners during the 1970s. On the other hand, the Salim Group's private resources were exploited by the state for general purposes. This is the case of the Cold Rolling Mill Indonesia Utama, a steel factory established in 1983 by Liem who, when requested by the government, was able to raise over $550 million in foreign loans and obtain the assistance of US Steel in the factory's management. It seems difficult to believe that Liem would have voluntarily chosen this notoriously unprofitable sector. Clearly, given his privileged position and government interventions favourable to him – by means of pricing and protection in other sectors – this move 'can only be fully understood in the context of his value and function as an instrument of government policy in sectors normally not commercially attractive' (Robinson 1986: 314). In sum, it is possible to suggest that, under particular conditions, the family firm reveals itself as the best device to fulfil immediate goals of industrial and economic policies (see, for instance, the declarations by Indonesian policymakers collected in Chalmers and Hadiz 1997).

The relevance of the institutional framework in explaining the long-lasting orientation toward the family firm becomes clear when comparing the cases of Japan and Italy. The two countries had a very similar history as late-industrialisers, with a strategic function pursued by the state in fostering the process. From the beginning, an important role was played by family firms in both countries: in Japan the first industrial revolution saw the emergence of the large, diversified, multi-subsidiary *zaibatsu*, in general (with some exceptions – see Morikawa 2001: 40) wholly controlled by a family holding. Meanwhile, in Italy the industrialisation process was made possible thanks to state intervention complemented by large universal banks sustaining private entrepreneurs and families. The outcome was, in both cases, an ownership structure of private large corporations concentrated in the hands of a minority of individuals and families who could multiply their power of control thanks to the use of various devices, such as financial holdings and pyramidal groups (see the essays by Kunio Suzuki and Franco Amatori in Shiba and Shimotani 1997). This situation came to an end after the Second World War. In Japan, the American anti-*zaibatsu* policies quickly brought about the dismantling of the large family groups (Morikawa 2001: 70ff.). The already-existing managerial hierarchies were, however, soon able to rebuild a complex ownership structure (*keiretsu*) based upon cross-shareholding and a main bank exerting a supervision role over the management (Morikawa 1997; Bernstein 1997). This created the basis for the country's astonishing economic upsurge from the 1970s onward. In the case of Italy, the 'Americanisation' process of the industrial system had to face both a dramatic shortage of financial capital in the private sector and the pervasive but necessary presence of the state as entrepreneur. The complex post-war political situation caused the country to delay the necessary reforms of antitrust laws, financial markets regulation, and commercial codes. The need for political stability and a rapid economic recovery in the face of the danger of Communism caused the Americans to give up their programmes of reform for Italian capitalism, which remained in the end based upon large pyramidal groups controlled by the state (by means of agencies such as IRI (Istituto per la Ricostruzione Industriale / Institute for Industrial Reconstruction) in manufacturing or ENI (Ente Nazionale Idrocarburi / National Agency for Gas and Oil) in energy). Also, families made extensive use of leverage to maintain their control of the corporation with the minimum of direct financial effort (Bianchi, Bianco, and Enriques 2001).

In Japan family control was eliminated by an 'institutional shock' and a national version of managerial capitalism. In Italy, however, no such transformation took place. In the large, private corporations, family control remained the rule and the development of adequate managerial hierarchies was very slow (Amatori 1997a: 270ff.; Barca, Iwai, Pagano, and Trento 1998: 37).

Culture

It is necessary to bear in mind that the institutional and legal environment in which family businesses operate is the product of a complex historical process moulded by culture, at both a local and national level. In his *Culture's Consequences*, Geert Hofstede defines culture 'as the interactive aggregate of common characteristics that influence a human group's response to its environment' (Hofstede 1980: 25). It is clear that attitudes toward business and 'economic rationality' must be set into this general framework. Take for instance the European perspective on enterprise in comparison with the American one. In the latter case the managerialisation process and growth imperatives have been facilitated, to some extent, by an entrepreneurial philosophy that considers the enterprise as a *commodity*, so that it can be sold or bought or placed on the market. The European point of view tends, on the contrary, to identify the enterprise with a *community*, i.e., there is an identity between the family (also considered in an extended way) and the economic activity, given the expectation that the enterprise will generate employment and welfare for the family, while the family is the primary source of finance, labour, and knowledge for the enterprise itself (about this distinction see Albert 1991; Hau 1995: 44). An immediate consequence of this was the diffusion of paternalism which reproduced in manufacturing the social relations typical of the agricultural world. In the European perspective paternalism in a broader sense refers to the creation of an 'internal work community' shaping all the relationships inside the enterprise. In this way the modern family firm was a tentative restatement of the traditional values of the bourgeois *Gemeinschaft*. Immediately obvious is the parallel with another apparently successful model of production organisation, namely the Japanese one, where feudal loyalty relationships are reproduced in an enterprise to which employees are committed by a strong sense of community and membership (Miller 1981: 7–11).

The history of *Bon Marché*, the French department store, provides a good illustration of this philosophy. Founded by the Boucicaut family in 1869, it was for several decades the most important French enterprise in distribution, if not the largest retail firm in the world. Zola described it in his novel *Au bonheur des dames*. After the founder's death in 1877 the *Bon Marché* went under the direction of his widow, Marguerite, who proved to be a skilful manager until her death in 1887. The Boucicauts not only committed themselves to creating a successful and profitable enterprise, but also managed quite successfully to establish a 'paternalistic' enterprise in the sense described above. This extended to all levels, from the lowest to the middle and top managers (Miller 1981: 77ff.). The enterprise was seen as an extended 'family' business (a *grande famille*), especially by the top executives who also became partners when Madame Boucicaut transformed the legal status of the company in 1880 to that of *société en commandite*. The result of this strategy was that, long after the death of the founder and of his wife, the *Bon Marché* remained a closed family firm of sorts, and this spirit carried over into the personal lives of the directors, their associates, and the principal shareholders. Intermarriage does not appear to have been uncommon (1981: 137–8).

In general, the European view is one of a long-term relationship between the enterprise and the family, the former being established not only for the present but for future generations. The consequence is 'familialism', i.e., the tendency to associate members of the family at any level – and often on a very strict kinship basis – with the allocation of resources, power, and responsibilities. In the Italian case, whereas dynasties have been one of the dominant elements in the industrialisation process, one interesting study published at the end of the 1970s pointed to a link between family ownership and certain common negative characteristics, such as low degrees of diversification, scant internationalisation, and poor managerial structures, especially where the quality of management was evaluated on the basis of loyalty rather than on performance levels (Pavan 1973). Other researchers have referred to 'amoral familialism' as the dominant characteristic of Italian business. They label the Italian tendency to give priority and privilege to family members and to the extended community (see Banfield 1958), even though this kind of behaviour has been present all over Europe for generations. A clear example of this 'convergence' in the dynastic motive is given by the essays published in the two issues – 9 (1995), and 12 (1996) – of *Entreprises et Histoire* edited by F. Crouzet and devoted to the theme 'Dynasties d'entrepreneurs'.

In explaining the long-lasting resilience of Greek family firms, Margarita Dritsas (1997: 90) provides striking evidence of the consequences both for the economic system and for the structure of the firms, of culture, ideology, and institutions:

In Greece, the dominant culture has traditionally upheld the pre-eminence of the family, linked with the concept of private property à la grecque (small family property, to be exact) which had been institutionalised by the Constitution . . . On the economic level it endorsed attitudes towards moderate wealth accumulation . . . it contributed to the maintenance of a traditional attachment to land, to local culture and particularistic practices . . . small family property and business became sacrosanct for the average Greek citizen.

Another important feature of the identification between family and firm – which in turn is 'culture's consequence' – concerns the use of resources. It is, in fact, undeniable that families have tended to exploit the resources of the enterprise by pursuing the goal of personal enrichment. It is also true, however, that this is not a critical issue in relation to large-sized firms. As suggested above, family firms tend to be as efficient in the use of resources as managerial firms, particularly in regard to long-term investments. The enrichment of the members of the dynasty should not be seen as the principal weakness of the family firm, even if it is frequently blamed for, and considered to be one of the main determinants of, family firms' decline.

As far as the issue of resources is concerned, the 'embeddedness' of the family and the firm in European culture is much more relevant in another aspect, i.e., the tendency historically displayed by entrepreneurs to expand their activity only when new resources (financial, but especially human, capital) become available. In this way, the enlargement of the firm's activity is often made possible only when the family can provide sufficient resources. This applies, for example, to the well-known case of the multinational activity in family firms in the Dutch food industry during the nineteenth century (Sluyterman and Winkelman 1993). An interesting recent doctoral study shows that patterns of expansion and succession in the most important multinational firms in the Low Countries were planned taking into account supplies of human capital, enhanced by marriage strategies (Arnoldus 2002). In his recent research on British trading companies in the nineteenth and twentieth centuries, Geoffrey Jones has demonstrated that the origins of multinational activity are to be found in the complex web of partnerships established by British merchant families all over the world. Trade houses and agencies remained as substantial family affairs well into the nineteenth and twentieth centuries, even when incorporation was common among trading and commercial activities. The family was the top level for decision-making even if, given the geographic dispersion of the partnership, it was necessary to employ managers or directors. In any case, these extra-familial managers would serve for a very long time – perhaps in a lifetime of employment in the company (Jones 2000: 52, 196, 207ff.). In any event, the family was the ultimate guarantee against unfaithfulness and unauthorised speculation (Jones 2000: 217). As an essential device to reduce information and transaction costs, the family subsequently drove the company expansion strategies (Casson 2000: ch. 6).

Undue generalisation can, however, be dangerous. Cultural attitudes have shaped both the significance of the family firm *inside* each national economy and also the organisational form taken by the enterprise itself and its management style. This has produced considerable differences from case to case. Take for instance the Asian experience which has been widely researched from the perspective of culture, family and social values. East Asian recent industrialisers have been able to transform their economies during the last decades and experience impressive and sustained rates of growth (Rose 1995b: xiv). For a long period, the upsurge of these economies was identified with the Japanese pattern of growth, emphasising significant differences between Western and Eastern management philosophies (Chen 1995: ch. 2, extensively drawing on Lodge and Vogel 1987: 2ff.). The 'collective philosophy' stemming from Confucianism and neo-Confucianism has been characterised as the primary influence on the economic organisation of East Asian societies (Redding 1990: 43ff.) and as an asset, especially when compared to Western 'Weberian individualism'.

Families, firms, and ideologies

In this way, one country's 'ideology' – defined as a set of beliefs employed to justify the actions of a country's institutions (Chen 1995: 309) – becomes a source of competitive advantage, as the Asian story demonstrates (Lodge and Vogel 1987; Thurow 1992). The Asian case is, however, only apparently homogeneous in this respect. National differences become evident, for example, when the Chinese model is compared with the Japanese (Hamilton 1998: 181). In his seminal work on Chinese capitalism, Redding (1990) has stressed: 'The idea that the way managers see the world affects economic systems via the organisations those managers create . . . this is especially so when the managers are owners at the same time. It is even more so when they come from a society with a strong set of values about co-operation and authority' (1990: vii). The Chinese concept is thus much more 'familialistic' than the Japanese one. A person is perceived to exist only in terms of his immediate family network, which means that: 'The families remain the basic survival units, that they are largely self-sufficient, that they do not fuse naturally into a general community, that they are fundamentally competitive, and that their members are largely motivated by the pragmatic exigencies of protecting and enhancing the family resources on which they in turn are highly dependent' (1990: 53). This has obvious implications for the organisational structure and management philosophy of overseas Chinese business enterprises when dynamic ASEAN countries such as Hong Kong, Singapore, Indonesia, Malaysia, the Philippines, and Thailand are considered. (For a complete survey on this issue in a historical perspective see Ampalavanar Brown 1995.) Family ownership and low trust result in an autocratic management style hostile to individual initiative and adverse to decentralised organisational forms that occur only when the family is able to control and manage diversification. In large East Asian firms, from Indonesian conglomerates to Korean *chaebols*, top and secondary key management positions were, and still are, reserved for relatives and family members, and the management style is authoritarian (Lee 1997).

The top 200 Indonesian corporations demonstrate some common features including diversification without formal co-ordination, extensive use of networking with other groups of Chinese origin in ASEAN countries (from the perspective of both finance and production), business beginnings rooted in trading and commerce, and very close relationships with the established political powers. All of them, with very few exceptions, are under family control so that strategic management positions are in the hands of a family, or very close relatives (Robinson 1986: ch. 9). In the Indonesian Salim Group, until the second half of the 1980s, there had not been any holding company at the head of the group, and the highly differentiated activity of the conglomerate was not under a formal co-ordination. Since the early nineties, the entire group has been formally controlled by a family holding (the Chairman of which is Liem Sioe Liong, with Andree Salim, his youngest son, as Vice Chairman, and Anthony Salim, the successor, as President and CEO). Day-to-day management of the eleven divisions (encompassing more than 450 companies) is carried out by professionals, mostly Chinese, co-ordinated directly by the Liem family (Sato 1993). The central role of the family has been accompanied by co-operation and networks, both of which have been instrumental in sustaining Chinese expansion abroad (Redding 1990: 33ff.).

In Japanese business history the family undoubtedly played a strategic role from the Meiji Restoration onwards; the family concept in Japan is, however, slightly different from the Chinese one. In the Japanese case, Confucian philosophy is much more pervasive; the family is *not* defined in biological terms but 'as those contributing to the economic welfare of the group, or *ie.*, irrespective of lineage. Moreover, in Japan collective values override the interests of the individual whether applied at the level of the family, the firm, or the nation' (Rose 1995b: xviii). The history of the *zaibatsu* is significant in this respect. Notwithstanding the fact that Japan is alone among the Asian countries in having applied primogeniture well before the Second World War, the ownership structure of the large, diversified concerns was based upon a family holding that controlled the enterprises belonging to the group. Managerialisation was, however, already in progress, in some cases already from the late Tokugawa period. In such instances salaried managers (*bantô*) were delegated by the family to manage the enterprises of the group (Yasuoka 1984a: 92; Yamamura 1978: 238ff.). The managerialisation of the *zaibatsu* was even more advanced during the period between the two World Wars, when the families remained simple shareholders in the holding company while 'salaried managers, who moved up the company's hierarchy through internal promotion, grasped real managerial control of the company' (Takeda 1999: 94). In formal terms, families reigned but did not govern (Morikawa 1997), even if other scholars prefer to delay until the end of the Second World War the transition from personal to managerial capitalism in Japan. The transition toward a managerial system was facilitated by culture and legitimated by a peculiar concept of 'family' which is based not only upon consanguinity but also on adoption:

The Japanese hardly distinguish between the two meanings. But the succession of the property in Japan is often based upon the concept of *ie.*, according to which the heir of a property is not necessarily a family member by blood. A successor in *ie.*, can be described as a successor of the role. The main objective of *ie.*, succession is to protect and expand the wealth of the family led by a capable individual rather than to bequeath the wealth only to blood-related family members.

(Chen 1995: 167)

In this way, in the case of the *zaibatsu*, the closest relatives were not expected to provide the top management of the concern itself, since the separation of ownership and management was functional to the well-being of the extended family enterprise. This structure revealed itself to be relatively efficient under pressure. Salaried managers were, in fact, the main actors in the vast process of restructuring, which made it easy to transform the old *zaibatsu* into the *keiretsu* after the post-1945 American occupation. The loss of power by the families did not mean that business groups lost organisational and managerial capabilities, since the holding company structure was replaced by a system of cross ownership among the companies belonging to the *keiretsu*, clustered around a financial core, or main bank (Morikawa 2001: 75–6).

If the long-term survival of a firm is generally due to its ability to adapt to changes in the external environment, this is especially true for family firms. In this case, however, family control plays an ambiguous role, sometimes facilitating and at other times hindering such adaptations. In other words, a family firm is the product of a specific national culture. The most successful examples of long-lasting family firms are those in which the relationship between property and management has been able to adapt to a changed environment and where the ownership structure has not turned into an obstacle to the firm's competitive strength. The issue of adaptation to growth and response to external pressure is relevant in studying the strengths and weaknesses of family capitalism. In a dynamic perspective it is clear that in those industries where size constitutes a key advantage, the family firm will be competitive if the owners are willing to undertake the necessary changes and to evolve from mere 'entrepreneurs' to 'organisational builders'. This issue is typically a cultural one, implying a radical transformation in the entrepreneurial role itself.

The major changes in this respect are those introduced by the second industrial revolution (at the end of the nineteenth century), and later, after the Second World War, by the third industrial revolution (Chandler 1994). During this period the entrepreneurial role was for the first time seriously put under pressure and transformed, in that manufacturing firms underwent substantial changes in their nature, while new governance structures as alternatives to direct entrepreneurship began to emerge. Together with family firms and partnerships, a new form, the public corporation, began to dominate in capital-intensive industries. From Berle and Means onward, the argument has been that these two organisational forms have been implicitly assumed as alternatives in the sense that the rise of the modern, public corporation coincided with the decline of the family firm, at least in the capital-intensive industries.

A more complete understanding of the evolution of the family firm and of the presence of this organisational form in the advanced and capital-intensive industries can be achieved by examining closely the transformation in the firms' structure that was brought by the second industrial revolution.

3
Family firms in the era of managerial enterprise

Almost fifty years ago, in her seminal work on the theory of the growth of the firm, Edith Penrose addressed the problem of the organisational complexity of the firm by pointing out the need for a definition of exactly what a big firm is (Penrose 1959: 17–19). She then introduced the distinction between 'entrepreneurial versus managerial competence'. For Penrose, a firm is not by its nature committed to growth. It is the entrepreneur's desire for profit and power, associated with technological evolution and market expansion, that pushes him (or her) to build up a large organisation based upon administrative efficiency. Thus, even if firms 'have been operating successfully for several decades under compctent and even imaginative management', they do not fully achieve the opportunities for expansion, since their owners 'have been content with a comfortable profit' and, above all, 'have been unwilling to ... raise capital through procedures that would have reduced their control over their firms' (1959: 34). Very good entrepreneurs as well as hard-working, creative managers have in this way often been an obstacle to a firm's growth, simply because their principal motivation was not profit-making and they did not fully exploit the firm's resources by, for example, searching for new products or markets.

In Penrose's perspective, however, the entrepreneurial factor is the 'residue' explaining the initial success of a firm in terms of versatility (imagination, timing, and so on), fund-raising (the ability to obtain financial resources during the initial stages of the activity), and ambition (1959: 39ff.). The quality of these 'entrepreneurial services' is absolutely critical in enhancing the managerial competence of a firm. For Penrose, the development of large and efficient organisations had to be based upon these criteria.

Which role for family firms? The traditional view

Penrose's theorisation helps to introduce the central point of this section. The big businesses of the second and third industrial revolutions in capital- and research-intensive industries underwent rapid and profound changes after their initial entrepreneurial stages. 'Empire' or 'goodwill' builders, as the founders of the giant corporations in steel, oil, chemicals, and pharmaceuticals were labelled (Penrose 1959: 39), were able to transform themselves into 'organisation builders', given the necessity to expand the scale and scope of their enterprises as a consequence of the transformation of production and distribution techniques. Organisation-building meant a radical transformation in the nature of the firm through the adoption of bureaucratic managerial structures. It also, however, indicated a growing consciousness on the part of the founders that the separation of ownership from control was unavoidable, and that they had to share the control of their enterprises with major shareholders, the representatives of institutional investors, and banks. In this way, the corporation separated itself from the personality of its founder and from the founding family that had provided the name and initial resources of the firm in terms of finance, labour, and management. As Glenn Porter put it for America:

In reality, the generation of giants (the lords of creation, Frederick Lewis Allen called some of them) acted as midwives in the birth of the modern corporation. Their achievements were great, their talents considerable, and their fortunes enormous . . . The impersonal, institutional demands of giant firms shaped new patterns of ownership and management by the opening years of the twentieth century, eclipsing the brief but exceedingly bright glow of the generation whose names had for a time symbolized big business.
(Porter 1993: 23)

In this framework it is clear that there was little room for the persistence of family firms. The onset of the managerial revolution meant that engineers, lawyers, and insider-trained personnel began to be appointed for senior positions, whether they were members of the founding family or not (Galambos 1983).

The process of financial disclosure on the part of the corporation, through which the firm was no longer dependent only on self-financing or the personal fortune of the owner, brought into the organisation new criteria and appointment procedures. This led ultimately to the elimination of the family as the main source of human capital. The corporation was a 'public' good, with thousands of owners and sometimes without a 'main' shareholder. It thus ceased to be, legally and practically, a private holding of a family whose members expected by right to be employed in the business. It was not only a matter of dimension: the enterprise became a completely new thing, from both the strategic and organisational perspective, compelling economists to build a new theoretical framework to investigate it. Going back to Penrose, 'there is no reason to assume that as the large firms grow larger and larger they will become inefficient; it is much more likely that their organisation will become so different that we must look on them differently; we cannot define a caterpillar and then use the same definition for a butterfly' (Penrose 1959: 19).

On the other hand, it is worth considering that the transformation of the corporation and the process of delegation of responsibility to management is a very difficult, complex process that is subject to several forces, among which are the attitudes and personality of the founder. In several cases the dialectic between the dynastic motive and the need for managerial hierarchies and delegation processes resulted in a progressive loss of competitive strength, which in turn challenged the firm's position in the market. Examples of these reversions crowd the history of modern industrial development in the advanced countries. This is, for instance, the story of Ford, an enterprise that from its beginnings depended on the personality and ideas of the founder, who in 1919 re-bought all the ordinary shares of the company, transforming it from public to personal and private again. According to Thomas McCraw and Richard Tedlow, this 'proved to be a fateful move. It put this vast company entirely under the personal control of one eccentric individual' (McCraw and Tedlow 1997: 272ff., 278). In the twenties the enterprise, after the firing of most of the management – most of whom flew to the main competitor, Alfred Sloan's General Motors (GM) – adopted a 'flat' organisational structure, headed and controlled by an ageing Henry Ford (he was in his seventies during the thirties), who was unwilling to delegate responsibilities to his capable son, Edsel. The result was a continuous loss of market share to the main competitor, GM – where Sloan was carrying out a vast reform of the organisational structure, introducing the M-form. During the period between the two World Wars, GM gained the pole-position in the industry. The situation at Ford came to an end only after the Second World War, when Edsel's son, Henry Ford II, became CEO and hired a skilful cohort of young top executives (McCraw and Tedlow 1997: 288).

Probably the best example of a difficult and failed transition from family firm to managerial enterprise is that of Siemens in Germany. From the beginning of the Siemens story the family played a strategic role in reducing uncertainty and promoting the growth of the company. Siemens' three main branches in Germany, Russia, and Great Britain were headed by the three Siemens brothers (respectively, Werner, Carl, and William), and this facilitated the integration and co-ordination of the multinational firm's activity (Kocka 1971). The family character of Siemens was also an important element shaping the whole organisation of the corporation. This extended to the relationships between labour and capital which were conceived as paternalistic and collaborative instead of adversarial. Under the leadership of Werner Siemens, however – who himself was conscious that a transition toward a decentralised form of authority was absolutely necessary – the German group was unable to transform its organisational form. The ownership structure remained strictly familial, even if, after 1897, under the pressure of the banks, it took the form of a joint-stock company. As a main consequence, Siemens proved to be unable to face the competitive pressure presented by the already managerial AEG (Kocka 1999: ch. 3). With Werner Siemens's retirement at the beginning of the new century, his son Wilhelm took over the leading responsibilities, promoting (largely thanks to the unchallenged authority of the Siemens name) new managerial hierarchies.

The relationship between the dynastic motive and the growth of the firm is particularly important in the history of another main German industrial concern, the Thyssen steelworks. August Thyssen founded Thyssen & Co. in 1871, and the firm began to grow rapidly after 1880 in consequence of the diversification of production and vertical integration (Fear 1997: 187). The founder, who had three sons and one daughter, however, was not conditioned in this case by familialism and dynastic motive. Thyssen had divorced in 1872, just a year after having founded his enterprise, and his relationships with his children were difficult (1997: 205).

This certainly had an influence on his managerial style, which was different from that of other empire builders of his time. More than just a classic entrepreneur, Thyssen became a modern corporate executive at the head of a hierarchy of professional salaried managers. Throughout his life, he generally identified more with his managers than with members of his own family (1997: 189).

The contrast between the family firm's structure and the requirements of growth, from both the financial and the organisational points of view, become generally apparent under the pressure of changes in the structure and dimensions of demand and consumption. Frequently in these cases the mixture of familial culture and paternalism, which had often successfully determined the firm's development, revealed itself to be a powerfully negative element. The Italian case is particularly significant in this respect. After the Second World War the country started its definitive modernisation, reaching an impressive rate of economic growth. The whole economic apparatus was consequently put under pressure, especially in capital-intensive industries, both publicly and privately owned. The rapid growth in demand and the transformation in consumption habits and standards profoundly challenged the old organisational models of the main Italian private corporations, still characterised by family-based ownership and managerial structures. In some cases, for instance that of Fiat, the transition from a family-owned to a managerial enterprise with large-scale production was undertaken very quickly and firmly: large investments in production culminated in the building of the extensive plant at Mirafiori, near Turin, where at the beginning of the 1950s Fiat began the mass production of small cars. Though control of the company was securely in the hands of the Agnelli family, it was at that time under the direction of Vittorio Valletta, a former top manager who, after the founder's death in 1945, became CEO. Giovanni Agnelli's son, Edoardo, had died in a plane crash in 1935 and his two sons, Gianni and Umberto, were too young to take effective roles in the firm's management. Valletta's successful strategy was to carry on scale-intensive production of small, cheap cars and to fulfil a rapidly growing demand. Valletta's policies of development were not obstructed by the family which, on the contrary, sustained the skilful top manager (who never purchased a single share in Fiat, declaring his desire to carry on the business *in loco parentis*, i.e. as a guardian) at the head of the company. In 1966 Gianni Agnelli, the nephew of the founder, took over the responsibility of the firm's management together with his brother Umberto (Castronovo 1999: 921ff.).

In the same industry and in the same period, however, the family could also reveal itself as the main barrier to the growth and modernisation of the firm, with adverse consequences for its market competitiveness. During the 1930s, at the death of its founder, Lancia was, after Fiat, the largest Italian car producer, well-known abroad for the high quality of its automobiles. The founder's widow, Adele, took over the responsibility of the firm's management, aided by a number of technicians and executives already working in the company. In 1948, however, the young (he was only twenty-four) Gianni, the founder's only son, became CEO of the company, which was facing the difficult transformation in the Italian car market of the period after the Second World War. Meanwhile, at Fiat, Valletta was pursuing his policy of growth, investment, and expansion, whilst Lancia chose to maintain its family character with its commitment to high-quality, craft-based products. Gianni invested a large amount of the company's financial resources in an expensive racing team – considered one of the best means of advertising – and refused funding from the European Recovery Plan so as to maintain Lancia's independence. The result was a progressive decline of the company, unable either to restructure in favour of mass production of small cars or, relying on its positive experience in racing, to focus on sports-cars as a profitable niche in competition with its famous rival, Ferrari (Amatori 1996: ch. 3).

We declare that our Company has to keep the primacy which it has maintained over the years . . . but our Company has, first of all, to be alive, and for this it is not necessary for it to grow excessively . . . I know very well that there are a lot of financiers willing to take over the Rinascente . . . I would consider the sole cause of the failure of myself, as a man and as a worker, to be obliged in the future to leave the control of the Company to a financial institution . . . .

(Amatori 1989: 206)

These words, pronounced by Aldo Borletti, the President and son of the founder of La Rinascente (during the 1950s and 1960s the most important Italian department store), controlled and managed by the two families Borletti and Brustio, capture very well the sharp contrast between the pressures coming from the market and the traditional ownership and organisational structures based upon family and kinship.

In sum, the second industrial revolution made evident, with an intensity never known before, the separation between capital-intensive industries and the light, traditional ones. In light industry the optimal size of the firm continued to be consistent with non-bureaucratic organisations in which the limited family resources proved ideal. The rate of diffusion of the family firm remained in this way relatively high, for instance, in textiles, light and specialised mechanics, machinery, shoemaking, and in some branches of the food and beverages industry. In other cases, such as building – where the structure of the production process was dominated by discontinuity, variability, and flexibility rendering the introduction of bureaucracy impossible – subcontracting, networking, and family partnerships persisted as the dominant organisational form.

In recent research on American specialised producers from the second half of the nineteenth century until the twenties and thirties (Scranton 1997), Philip Scranton suggests that the growth of big business has been accompanied all along by the creative presence of specialised producers. These persistent actors have been untouched by the technological imperatives of mass production. The specialised producers – furniture-makers, hosiery-makers, ship-builders, machine-tool-makers – and the enterprises that were 'in the middle', between specialised and mass production (e.g. iron and steel rolling mills, men's clothing, boots and shoes, autos and parts, and others listed in Scranton 1997: table 3), have been a significant element in American industry, contributing from one-third to one-half of the whole value added at the beginning of the twentieth century. These specialised producers were a relevant component of the whole productive system, as it was these firms that manufactured the machinery for the scale-intensive corporations. Yet, the specialised producers were also able to fulfil a differentiated and variable demand coming from the middle and the upper classes, especially in products such as home furnishings and clothing. The organisation of the production process was the opposite of that in capital-intensive industries. In his study of the US textile industry from the beginning of the nineteenth until the first half of the twentieth century, Scranton also pointed to the considerable difference between the production system in Philadelphia and that in use in Lowell, Massachusetts, which was based upon large-scale, unskilled work and standardised production for the mass market (Scranton 1983 and 1989). The 'proprietary capitalism' in Philadelphia was on the contrary less capitalised, based upon small and medium-sized specialised firms employing a skilled workforce. The production process was based on networking and flexibility, specialised machinery, and personal knowledge among the entrepreneurs who sold on the basis of the quality of their goods, and not on that of the average cost per unit.

Scranton does not examine the ownership structures of the firms he discusses. However, his research suggests that the pattern of manufacturing organisation present in the Philadelphia textile industry was widely based on the individual and family business. Clearly, this form of enterprise was consistent with the particular kind of production, which had to be flexible and variable, entrepreneurial and not bureaucratic. The family firm's diffusion is explained not only by technical considerations (i.e., the small and medium size of the production units), but also by the fact that it was the most suitable form of management organisation under specific conditions. For instance, the high degree of skill required both in the workforce and in the entrepreneur implies a method of training and knowledge transmission that is at best performed in the family circle, where competence and sensibility is, as Marshall would say, in the 'atmosphere'. Flexibility implies also a high degree of risk, both from the productive and from the financial points of view. The family is not only a reservoir of skill, labour, and know-how. As Charles Sabel and Jonathan Zeitlin (Sabel and Zeitlin 1985 and 1997) suggest in the context of their historical alternatives to mass production theory, in the Philadelphia textile industry the identification between the family and the enterprise was functional to this particular kind of specialised production well into the era of capital intensity. In other words, the flexibility required in these industries can be achieved only through a 'de-verticalisation' of the production process, since the relationships among the different producers have to be as variable as are the changes in demand and in the market's requirements. From this perspective, the family is embedded into the local system of values and culture and is an institution that grants an efficient exchange of information, reducing the transaction costs among the various producers. In the case of the Roubaix textile industry, David

Landes (1976) along with Sabel and Zeitlin emphasises the role of the *système Motte* in shaping the competitive strength and the configuration of the production process in the district. This system was based upon networks of local producers, very specialised and knowledgeable, who were interconnected by kinship and high-trust ties, thus ensuring the necessary flexibility to compete with mass production. According to Alfred Motte, the entrepreneur who explicitly outlined the project around the mid nineteenth century, it was necessary to pair each family member who had come of age with an experienced technician from one of the family's firms; they were then provided with start-up capital (most of which was held, of course, by the family member) in order to establish a company that specialised in one of the phases of production that was still needed. The new firms often found markets outside, as well as inside, the family, but their financial and emotional ties to the lineage made them dependable partners, even in difficult times. This common loyalty to the family freed the companies to make the realignments dictated by changing fashions, whilst ensuring against extreme fluctuations in the demand for particular processes: it also provided the necessary trust to maintain a system of common financial reserves, marketing and purchasing (Piore and Sabel 1984: 34–5).

The history of the Italian industrial districts presents the best example of the role of the family as an institution. These districts can be defined as clusters of small and medium-sized enterprises active in one industry, each performing one or more phases of the production process, usually linked by informal agreements and debt or credit connections. In their purest form, the relationships among the entrepreneurs are informal, not contractual, and based upon trust and a widely shared system of values and culture. The networks linking the enterprises are variable according to the often very rapid changes imposed by the market. Examples of this kind of production organisation are to be found almost exclusively in the light, traditional industries in which the production process is fragmented and its single phases can be efficiently performed by different producers. This is the case, for example, in shoemaking, in various branches of textile and clothing manufacturing as well as in the mechanical and machine-tools industries. It is also prevalent in the production of a large number of luxury goods (Goodman and Bamford 1989; Cossentino, Pyke, and Segemberger 1996).

The point worth stressing here is related to the nature and ownership structure of the single production unit: small, entrepreneurial, and owned and directed by the family, which is the main source of labour, skill, finance, and personal contacts. The kinship relations among the entrepreneurs act together with the personal connections in enhancing trust and knowledge, reducing transaction costs. The standing of a family inside the local society, and also the relations between its members and the wider community, are essential to the circulation of credit and information at the local level (Dei Ottati 1994; Colli 1998).

The family also provides the necessary flexibility in the use of labour. As happens in a peasant society – which these local systems frequently originate from and remain firmly rooted in – each member of the household is involved in the production process when necessary. Inside the local production systems, the overexploitation of the family members is fairly accepted and frequent. The role of women, for instance, even if frequently obscure and hidden, is a key resource for these entrepreneurs, who are often able to start up their firms only thanks to the aid of their wives, sisters, or mothers, who provide active financial, administrative, and technical support.

Which role for the family firm? Toward a new perspective

The dualism introduced by the second industrial revolution between capital-intensive industries – concentrated, oligopolistic, and corporate – and the light sectors – small, entrepreneurial, and often engaged in single-phase and flexible production – should not be seen as too rigid. This dualism is rooted in the technological revolution of the late nineteenth century and is reflected in the ownership and organisational structures of the enterprises, creating an industrial world populated, according to Edith Penrose, by 'caterpillars and butterflies'. It is evident, however, that these two categories have to be considered as the extremes of a continuum rather than two completely separate worlds. In fact, if specialised producers can often employ complex bureaucracies (Scranton 1997: ch. 1), it is also not rare to find in scale-intensive industries the flat organisational structures modelled on the owner family.

The managerial era is, also in its post-Fordist and post-modern version, populated by family firms active not only in labour-intensive, low-tech industries at an artisanal level following the classic 'residual' model, but also in high-tech, capital-intensive, and sometimes scale-intensive industries. There are, along this continuum, a quantity of hybrids – organisational structures combining the logic and the advantages of the family firm as well as of bureaucratic and managerial organisations. Hybrids are perfectly rational and fit efficiently inside a defined cultural framework. Their existence can be explained only by considering them as the efficient product of particular institutional conditions, and not simply as a failure that should be corrected by a compulsory convergence process.

To illustrate this point two examples are particularly significant. The first one is given by the history of the Japanese *zaibatsu* before their dismantling after the Second World War. According to Hidemasa Morikawa, the evolution of these enterprise groups can be divided into three main phases (Morikawa 1992, and 2001: 47ff.). During the first of these, from the groups' origins until the end of the nineteenth century, the organisational structure of the groups was heavily based upon the family, which provided the human capital necessary to fill top- and middle-management positions. In some cases, after the Meiji Restoration, the lack of managerial skills in the family was resolved both by involving the closest relatives and by means of the *bantô*, a kind of 'ruler' governing in the name of the family, to which he was strictly linked by fidelity and respect. The *bantô*, who generally belonged to the *samurai* class, were, in Morikawa's view, more of an obstacle than an incentive to the corporation's development, given their autocratic, nepotistic, and conservative behaviour (1992: 47).

In other words, the presence of a factotum is not to be confused with the introduction of a modern managerial hierarchy, the essence of which is the devolution of power inside the organisation itself. In any event, the generation effect, together with the progressive enlargement of the scale and scope of the main *zaibatsu* activities, led to the introduction of salaried managers by the end of the nineteenth century, even if, in this case, it is still not possible to talk of a complete managerialisation process. In the case of Mitsui, for example, at the end of the nineteenth century the control of group subsidiaries was delegated to professionals, but the dynastic motive remained of extreme relevance at least until the 1930s (Morikawa 1992: 114ff.; 2001: ch. 3).

On the other hand, management was not completely free from its ties and moral obligations toward the property which still maintained a considerable control over strategic decisions. Haruhito Takeda, for instance, emphasises the fact that before the Second World War the families were still the main shareholders and maintained a complete control over the management decisions and over the governance of the whole corporation (Takeda 1999: 90). As the scope of the activities run by the whole concern grew, an organisational structure based on the multi-subsidiary system was preferred to the multi-divisional one. This meant the creation of a large number of top-management positions and hence a high degree of management motivation (Morikawa 1992: 189). In a third phase, however, a further separation took place between the family and the holding company of the *zaibatsu*. During the period between the World Wars, new cohorts of managers took over responsibility for running the relationships between the holding company and its subsidiaries, which were already under managerial control. In this way the family became increasingly separated from the day-to-day management of the concern. The holding company, however, was increasingly seen as 'a neutral zone for the co-ordination of the family's and management's interests', even if, in the end, the family maintained the authority to make major changes in the business, or to choose the top management (Takeda 1999: 95).

At the end of this process of transformation, and before their forced dissolution after the Second World War, the organisational and governance structure of the *zaibatsu* had evolved considerably. The families had given up a considerable part of their authority, especially in the day-to-day management of the corporation. Furthermore, the presence of a large network of subsidiaries had associated a high degree of management motivation (multiplying the top positions) with the possibility of raising considerable financial resources on the capital market. The holding company was the place where the negotiations between the family and top management took place, so that the policies and strategies of the corporation were not influenced by unattended intervention by the family. The presence of written codes of conduct also helped to maintain this separation.

The organisational form of the *zaibatsu* allowed it to maintain the positive aspects of the family business for long periods. In this respect, the qualities of loyalty and commitment, insiders' careful training, and above all the unwillingness to delegate power loomed large. The owner families were able to take a long-term view, appoint the most qualified personnel available on the market, diversify the original business, and progressively accept a loss of decision-making power in the day-to-day management in order to maintain their authority over the whole enterprise. The *zaibatsu* proved in the end to be an efficient form of corporate governance *inside* a particular cultural framework at a time when Japanese industrial capitalism faced serious internal and international challenges. As Morikawa suggests, in this situation 'a family business that was ruled by blood ties and family traditions and that refused to develop new enterprises or employ new talent put its very survival in jeopardy' (Morikawa 1992: 246).

The history of the Japanese *zaibatsu* provides an interesting case of family firms successfully active in capital- and scale-intensive industries in the managerial era. At the core of Morikawa's thesis is the idea that the large, diversified business groups were the best organisational form to compete in that particular period and in such an institutional and cultural context. The ability to cope with the challenges of growing competition, especially after the 1868 Restoration, by means of diversification and long-term investments in human capital consisted of maintaining a flexible organisation and balancing the virtues of both market-based and bureaucratic structures, entrepreneurial and managerial philosophies.

In a completely different context and historical period, the same conclusions can be obtained from the case of today's emerging dynamic, internationalised, medium-sized family firms that are able to dominate international market niches with very specialised products. The Italian case is particularly telling in this respect. From the 1980s onwards, a substantial process of restructuring took place inside the fragmented world of the established industrial districts. In several cases a process of 'hierarchising' took place, and bureaucratic or quasi-bureaucratic relations were substituted for the market mechanism proper of the industrial district in its pure form. Some major (if compared to the average dimension of the district's single unit) enterprises began to emerge at this time, and whilst they continued to be rooted in the local industrial district in terms of access to skilled labour, finance, and know-how, they progressively moved to larger-scale operations and more complex organisational forms.

The reasons behind this transformation are various. The critical factor was globalisation in the 1990s, which accelerated the inter-nationalisation process in medium-sized enterprises. These were often active in well-defined, international market niches – for instance, machine tools and other durable goods, clothing, luxury goods, and the other various branches of the so-called 'Made in Italy'. The growth resulting from these transformations was managed by the creation of hierarchical structures based upon a multi-subsidiary system. This was in some ways similar to that adopted by the Japanese *zaibatsu*. In the Italian case, a financial holding company heads a large number of subsidiaries, active on the home market and abroad.

These 'new' actors in the country's industrial landscape experienced steady and sometimes impressive rates of growth in terms of sales, value added, and in employees. There was also a growing internationalisation process that resulted in some cases in a remarkable dominance of world-sized market niches. Given the peculiar economic and industrial history of the country, these companies are now among Italy's top corporations, even if they still maintain the character of medium-sized, sometimes even small, enterprises active in traditional or specialised industries.

Probably the most representative case of one of these 'pocket multinationals', given its world-wide diffusion, is the Benetton group, an international leader in the fashion and clothing industry. There are many similar cases, very well known at an international level, for instance Ferrero (chocolate), Natuzzi (fittings and furniture), Luxottica (glasses), as well as the Armani and Versace groups. These corporations share a common history, generally going back to the 1950s and 1960s – decades during which the national economy experienced its most significant modernisation. Possessing an entrepreneurial ethos rooted in local systems of production, they have remained as strategic sources for subcontracting. The process of growth and internationalisation began generally during the 1980s and early 1990s, when an enlargement of the scope of the activity began.

Perhaps the most striking feature of these business groups lies in their governance and organisational structures. With very few exceptions, the recent history of these enterprises confirms the complete control of the family over the corporation. Often, the founder still directly manages all the strategic activities of the group, with only a small degree of decentralisation in the decision-making process, which is usually left to the heirs or to professional managers. Even these professional managers are sometimes co-opted, thanks to marriage strategies, or appointed after a long career inside the firm itself on the basis of personal knowledge and trust. In such a way it is possible to talk of 'driven democracy'.

The family's influence is reflected in the composition of the board, which is dominated by the founder's immediate family or close relatives. The family is, in many cases, the source of skill that has always been relied upon to provide finance, labour, and know-how. The structures of these groups mirror their historical evolution. The first, original nucleus of the enterprise has transformed itself into a family-controlled financial holding company, presiding over a large number of unincorporated subsidiaries active in the core, but also in very diversified fields. This is also consistent with vertical integration, a structure that sharply differentiates these middle-sized enterprises from the generality of Italian small business. The operative units (both productive and commercial) are run by relatives or very often by professionals strictly linked to the family. The family still, however, maintains control of the subsidiaries via their boards which generally contain several members of the controlling family.

In the case of the Benetton group, its history goes back to the 1950s when four siblings, Luciano, Carlo, Gilberto, and Giuliana Benetton started a small subcontracting activity in the hosiery industry. As with many other small workshops spread through the countryside near Treviso in the Venetian region, the business was strictly family-run from its inception. According to one of the firm's official 'biographies' (Mantle 1999), the original division of labour among family members was rigid. Luciano, the eldest of the four, together with his younger brother Gilberto, went around selling the hosiery that his sister, Giuliana – in turn helped by her mother –

produced at a knitting machine bought with loans from friends and relatives. The business idea was quite simple: to produce and sell hosiery of different colours instead of the traditional, single dark colours. At the beginning of the 1960s the small family workshop enlarged the scale of the activity and started to sell its products directly by means of a chain of shops at home and, from the beginning of the following decade, also abroad. From the seventies onward, this capillary distribution system grew rapidly due to the introduction of franchising contracts with small shopkeepers. This was accompanied by a production strategy based upon scale-intensity, low prices, and intense advertising. The flexibility required by the particular kinds of production was achieved successfully due to the presence in the region of an extended network of small subcontractors. At the beginning of the 1980s, the Benetton group was founded and in 1986 was listed on the Milan Stock Exchange. Today, the four siblings control a huge conglomerate, Edizione Holding, by means of a limited liability financial holding. The main interests are in the textile industry (with the vertically integrated Benetton Group) and in snacks and restaurants in the form of the Autogrill chain. The group is present all over Europe and the USA after the recent acquisition (1999) of Host Marriot Services. The size of the corporation is significant: at an aggregate level, sales in 1998 reached about 4.7 billion Euros, with around 30,000 employees.

The Benetton family, however, is not a mere owner; even if growth meant delegation, the key positions at the middle and lower levels are still in the hands of the four founders and their descendants, who hold managerial responsibilities in the group's subsidiaries.

In the case of Benetton, as in several other groups of smaller size, the family seems to have been able to coexist with professional management by building up an organisational structure where the virtues of family involvement are associated with the advantages derived from the delegation of responsibility into a multi-subsidiary structure. It is difficult – and probably beyond the goal of the work at hand – to say if this is destined to be an enduring solution or only a step toward a definitive separation between ownership and control.

In several circumstances, the scale and scope of the activity of middle-sized corporations do not imply a need for delegation and for the creation of a managerial hierarchy. Clearly, this has to do with a transformation in production techniques and in the market demand that some sectors, especially in consumer goods, have experienced during the last decades, shifting from a mere scale-intensive model to a growing product differentiation. The enlargement of the scope of the activity, instead of the scale, is clearly consistent with organisational growth based upon the multi-subsidiary system, which is perfectly consistent with a blend of family-based and managerial hierarchies.

From this perspective, and looking at stories similar to that of Benetton, it is possible to affirm that the traditional view of the role of the family firm in the era of managerial growth is almost reductive. As demonstrated, the family firm is neither the organisational form proper for small producers active in traditional, labour-intensive industries, nor simply a transient state on the way to more developed and sophisticated organisational forms. Even if in transformation, to the extent that it is the dominant organisational form in specialised and traditional industries, the family firm has proved to be resilient – adequate to cope with rapid shifts and changes in the market demand, and even maintaining a crucial dimension in terms of scale economies by means of the instrument of the multi-subsidiary group.

Old problems, open questions: leadership succession, corporate governance, and path dependence

The enduring role and resilience of the family firm in modern and even 'post-modern' industrial economies raise a number of questions that can be answered from a historian's point of view. These issues are relevant because family firms continue to constitute an important section of the economic system, not only in manufacturing, but also in services and finance. Undeniably in some cases, family firms today are *the* key sources of competitive advantage in rational industrial structures, and this makes them a crucial asset also at the *macro* level, given their contribution to overall economic growth. The Italian case is particularly telling in this respect; the family firm dominates the national industrial structure, proving also to be a very efficient, perhaps the most efficient, model, particularly in the case of medium-sized, specialised, and internationalised companies. If, however, the existence of the family firm is consistent with the turnover ratio typical of the industrial districts subject to a high number of 'births' and 'deaths' of entrepreneurial initiatives, this is not the case for world-wide specialised market niches. In this case the problems affecting the family firm can irremediably undermine its competitiveness resulting in a loss of market share to the benefit of other, very often foreign, competitors.

From the 1980s onward the focus of research on family firms has shifted progressively to the dynamics shaping the internal organisation of the single-family firm, its strategies, and competitive strength. Particular emphasis has been placed on the issue of leadership succession, which is increasingly perceived as the crucial issue affecting the family firm's welfare (Corbetta 2001: §3). This is particularly evident in those countries, for instance Italy or Spain, where family firms have particular relevance in sustaining the country's competitive advantage (on Spain, see Gallo and Pont 1988; Gallo 1995; Pérez 1997; on Italy, Amatori and Colli 2000). Even a superficial reading of specialist management literature, however, confirms that the passage of a business from a founder to his or her successor is likely to be fraught with difficulty in other geographical and cultural contexts as well (Alcorn 1982: 2; Dyer 1986: 3–13; Ayres 1990: 3–22). During the 1990s, an enormous amount of detailed research was produced on leadership succession by scholars of management and by consultants (for a synthesis, see, for instance, Dyer and Sanchez 1998), even if analysis from both a comparative and a historical point of view is still scarce (an attempt in this direction is that, for instance, by Pérez 2000 and by Colli, Pérez, and Rose 2001). Despite the obvious differences in the succession process in relation to history and culture, it is, however, possible to identify some useful generalisations (on this see Colli and Rose 2002, on which the following section largely draws).

Historically, the process of leadership transition has been influenced by the fact that the family provides protection against uncertainty, especially in rapidly changing environments. Yet this is also true when both the sphere of management and the choice of future leaders are concerned. Close networks of trust – from extended families to clans and business communities – ensure a combination of incentives, effective monitoring, and loyalty (Pollak 1985), and have traditionally been internal markets for managerial skills. This path of recruitment was the norm in all levels of British management up until the 1950s (Payne 1984; Chandler 1990a; Rose 1994; Rose 1998). In early nineteenth-century America, one legacy of Philadelphia's proprietary capitalism was a capacity to secure continued family control of businesses through the creation of spin-off firms to accommodate subsequent generations well into the twentieth century (Scranton 1993).

Even today the family business is synonymous with insider succession all over continental Europe, not least in Italy where 'the idea that a company is a personal or family domain seems to materialise as a persistent culture' (Amatori 1997a: 270). Meanwhile, in the new industrialising countries, in both Asia and Latin America, family succession remains the norm in the firmly entrenched business groupings (Strachan 1976; Leff 1978; Lansberg and Perrow 1991; Dutta 1996).

Family and business together often leads to deep contradictions, and consequently the process of change in business leadership may be problematic to the point of traumatic shock and genuine risk to the firm's survival (Rose 1993). Historical evidence supports this idea. In nineteenth-century Britain, as well as in twentieth-century Italy, although numerous forces, including inheritance laws and strong parental authority, led to a dynastic approach to business, there were often serious problems associated with creating continuity in family firms. This was the case when the heirs were unwilling or more often unable to take over the responsibility of the firm's management. It is here that the often-quoted 'Buddenbrooks effect', schematising the inadequacy of heirs to obtain the same success as the founder, gains some ground.

On the other hand, even when the new generation is willing to enter the business, a sharp conflict often arises from the introduction of new strategies and structures in an old, often sclerotic environment, especially when ageing business leaders are reluctant to retire. This introduces another relevant issue, i.e., that of succession planning and successors' training. Even if in this field there is a growing bulk of empirical research (for instance, the *Family Business Review* publishes yearly several contributions on the topic), there is still a distinct lack of information and investigation from a historical and comparative perspective (among the rare exceptions, see Scranton 1986; Rose 2001; Colli, Pérez, and Rose 2001).

According to existing research, however, formal planning of succession was rare in Britain and the United States, while it was comparatively more common in continental Europe (see, for instance, on France, Hau 1995: 57; on the Dutch case, Arnoldus 2002; on Spain, Pérez 1999). In the Italian case, the economic backwardness of the country and the will to industrialise during the second half of the nineteenth century encouraged the first entrepreneurs to manage the training of their heirs. This happened not only inside the firm but also by means of sending heirs abroad – particularly to France, Germany, and Britain, where they could learn the most recent technical innovations. For instance, looking at the history of the most important textile firms of the country, it is difficult to avoid the impression that the founders carefully planned their succession, mixing shop-floor training, technical studies, and travels abroad. Also today, in medium and large family firms, the issue of succession is a key issue, as many of the successful, world-wide and specialised market leaders were founded during the 1960s. Even if almost always familial, there is a growing trend toward careful planning of the succession, thanks also to the aid of professionals and consultants (Neubauer and Lank 1998).

The issue of succession becomes especially problematic where large numbers of heirs are concerned, and this has meant the formalisation of previously unwritten procedures regulating the change in the leadership and the hiring of family members. In the case of sibling partnerships or cousin consortiums it is necessary to regulate the relationship between the family, as a source of human capital and managerial competencies, and the firm. Similarly, the relationship between the members of the family who take an active entrepreneurial role in the firm and the other relatives who are outside the organisation must be regulated (Ward 1986; Lansberg 1999). Usually, the agreements signed among relatives take the form of written 'constitutions' (Neubauer and Lank 1998: 65) to which – as was the case of the Japanese *zaibatsu* – each family member involved in the firm is somehow committed.

The substitution of formal for informal rules has been accelerated recently, due to the pressure on the medium and large family firms coming from the disclosure and transparency required by national codes of corporate governance and by national and international financial markets. Although such constitutions and the use of formalised family meetings have increased in popularity in Europe, Latin America, and Australia in recent years, only a limited number of family firms in the Western world have maintained effective family meetings.

In a comparative perspective it should be noted that the problem of intergenerational conflict does not have the same relevance in all cultures. For example, the durability of family business in India over several generations has been explained in terms of a combination of distinctive attitudes toward the family and family members that minimise the degree of conflict (Dutta 1996).

Partially linked to the issue of leadership succession is that of corporate governance, which can be defined as a system of rules and structures by which companies are directed and controlled. By this mechanism corporations are monitored by the various stakeholders who share interests in the firm itself, from the shareholders to the employees, from the financial institutions to the customers.

The issue of corporate governance has been gaining ground during the last decade as well in the world of family business (Ward 1992; Neubauer and Lank 1998: 65ff.). This is especially the case when the family members are numerous – and not all involved in the firm's day-to-day management. Likewise, when seeking resources to finance expansion, former 'family dictatorships' have been forced to rely upon external capital – for example, by establishing long-term credit relations with a bank or by partially going public. In the case of family firms, the introduction of rules of governance often means a radical transformation of traditional management practices. This can result in increased transparency, for instance in accounting, reporting, and control procedures, as well as the disclosure of other, previously hidden kinds of information, e.g. the structure and duration of shareholders' voting agreements together with practices of protection of minority shareholders (Ward 1992).

The debate on corporate governance has been particularly widespread in Europe. In this case, with the noticeable exception of the United Kingdom, the family firm is present at almost every dimensional and sectoral level. The diversification of financial markets has resulted in a growing tendency to go public at all levels of firms, or at least to rely upon means of financing growth other than by internal resources or short-term debts (Whittington and Mayer 2000; Barca and Becht 2001).

In the case of the stock market, 'new' segments (such as the Neumarkt in Germany, the Star and Nuovo Mercato in Italy, and the Nouveau Marché in France) have made large amounts of financial resources available to small and medium-sized companies. Furthermore, the presence of regulatory authorities on the stock markets has forced the major companies – and among them a large number of companies owned and controlled by families – to establish 'codes of discipline' regulating the relationships among minority and majority shareholders and introducing greater transparency in relation to internal policies and strategies.

Changes in the traditional modes of conduct for medium and large family firms are noteworthy. In the Italian case, large family firms had obtained the resources necessary to finance their growth both through financial institutions and also via the stock market. However, this did not mean they became public companies *strictu sensu*; the founders and their families were able to maintain a real control over the firms in question, influencing their policies and strategies by means of various instruments. Among these had been the issuing of stocks with limited or no voting rights, the presence of shareholders' agreements, and above all the creation of pyramidal groups. By these means they have been able to control large amounts of capital with limited resources (Bianchi, Bianco, and Enriques 2001). In this framework, minority shareholders have a limited influence, and the families continue to dominate by appointing CEOs and top managers, thus defining the whole group's strategies. During the 1990s the most important Italian private groups were controlled by families (for instance, the Agnelli at Fiat) or individuals (Carlo De Benedetti at Olivetti) who, thanks to financial holdings and 'Chinese boxes' (as the financial pyramids are nicknamed in Italy), multiplied their power of financial control. The recent introduction of disclosure and transparency rules at the EU level (see, for instance, Becht 1997), together with a greater degree of compulsory regulation for the financial and stock markets, challenged deeply this consolidated system. For instance, in 1998 a consolidated finance Act introduced the regulation of shareholders' agreements, enhancing also the power of minority shareholders. This has resulted in families becoming more and more compelled to share their control with other agents, such as institutional investors, financial institutions, and also minority stockholders, who can exert much more influence over leadership succession strategies than in the past.

Both leadership succession and corporate governance issues are relevant aspects of a more general problem involving the values and culture of family firms in the rapidly changing environment of the globalisation era. The culture of individual family firms is a consequence of the aspirations of the founders and of their successors, which shape the firm's internal and external relationships and determine the way these change through time. In a rapidly evolving environment the presence of strong values and of a consolidated corporate culture are undoubtedly assets against uncertainty. On the other hand, this can result in inward- rather than outward-looking business cultures and firms can become almost impervious to change.

The preference for 'insider' succession in order to maintain internal stability can delay dynamism and innovation, the latter being more likely when firms recruit from outside. Individual history matters, but it can also become an obstacle to change, especially in organisations that are firmly committed to tradition and consequently hostile to change. Moreover, the long-term commitment of family shareholders – which can be an asset for the management in periods of crisis and turbulence – may contribute to the lock-in of the firm's strategies, since it fails to provide incentive to undertake new strategies for growth (Müller 1996: 44). The inextricable embeddedness of the family in its economic and social environment does not obviously help to avoid a risky path-dependence. It may indeed dull the firm's competitiveness, in terms of pursuing new markets and products, even if leadership succession in family firms means a 'leap' in the company's market approach.

There is abundant historical evidence that the long-term resilience of family-owned enterprises requires the ability to institute changes and the willingness to adapt the original business idea to new market circumstances. For instance, in the case of the two main Swedish family-owned business groups – Bonnier, involved in media and publishing from the 1840s, and Wallenberg, active in banking and manufacturing from the mid nineteenth century – the strong commitment to traditional family values accompanied the ability to adapt to change and develop new business ideas (Larsson, Lindgren, and Nyberg 2000). Similar conclusions are drawn in

Margrit Müller's research on two Swiss companies in the chemical and steel sectors from the mid nineteenth century to the present. In these cases, the long-lasting success of the enterprise was ensured not only by ability to adapt to changes in markets and technology, but also by the willingness of both of the families 'to loosen the links between the family and the firm' during the difficult period of the 1970s (Müller 1996: 44). In the French case, the stories of Peugeot and Michelin (Chadeau 1993) confirm that old industrial dynasties are also to be found in capital- and scale-intensive large corporations.

In the end it can be said that long-lasting family firms have been able to pursue strategies of survival based upon the continuous search for a compromise between the aspirations of the family members and the constraints imposed both by market competition and by institutional and legal systems. These agents have succeeded in a process of fine-tuning that combines the virtues of trust, low transaction costs, and long-term commitment with creative entrepreneurship and management.

4
Conclusions

During the last two decades of the twentieth century, family business has often been centre-stage in the debates surrounding organisational change in business. Analysis has matured from a defence of personal capitalism to the discussion of international variations in business capabilities generally and family firms in particular. The aim of this study is to stress the relevance of 'family business' in the long run as well as its resilience across place and time. Despite the convergence hypothesis, the family firm has been a critical element in the industrialisation process, from the first industrial revolution to the post-Fordist era. A significant number of family firms, in both specialised and scale-intensive industries, have proved able to adapt themselves to transformations in markets and technology whilst maintaining their leadership over time. If there is ample evidence of the so-called 'Buddenbrooks effect', there are also numerous examples of successful fourth-, fifth-, and also sixth-generation family firms.

This study has also stressed the extreme diversity of family businesses, which include a range of types from large, multinational and complex corporations to middle-sized specialised producers, as well as the small and atomised production unit inside an industrial district. One important point to note is that, despite the relevance of the subject, there is a surprising lack of theoretical, economic research, and even then the family firm is usually identified with the small and elementary production unit while the empirical work has often been written from a purely 'managerial' point of view (Casson 2000: 197). Whilst economic historians have investigated the family firm as a specific organisational form common during the early stages of the industrialisation process, in doing so they have generally avoided analysing its persistence through the second and third industrial revolutions, while disregarding any internationally comparative approach.

In its strictest definition, the family firm is fully owned and managed by family members and the social and economic identification between the two institutions is almost complete. It is clear, however, from the evidence presented here, that a more realistic definition would be wider, encompassing all cases in which the family maintains a share of the capital sufficient to appoint top management and influence the firm's strategies, thereby limiting the set of choices available to management.

This study has also emphasised that the notion that family firms remain constantly the same in every place and over time is an incorrect generalisation. Their resilience and efficiency, as well as their contribution to the wealth of the nation, depend also on the cultural and institutional environment shaping their organisational structures as well as the relationships between the family and the firm. Another generalisation that has been analysed here is the suggestion that the family firm is a transient form between the individual, entrepreneurial initiative and the managerial, publicly owned corporation. There is much evidence, on the contrary, to show that family firms are the most appropriate organisational form for the transmission of the founder's original aim to increase the family's and the firm's welfare.

One of the aims of this study has been to discuss the central issue of the persistence of family firms in modern advanced industrial economies. In the traditional interpretation, the family firm can successfully compete only in specialised, skill-based sectors and in those industries where transaction costs are comparatively high (Casson 2000: 203; Corbetta 2001). Although it is true that family firms were one of the engines of the industrial revolution, reducing transaction costs in a risky and uncertain environment, it is also possible to find successful examples of family-owned concerns operating in modern, scale-intensive industries. Furthermore, the traditional view does not explain why this organisational form is so common in modern developed economies even though information is easier to come by and laws and codes are more strictly enforced than in the past.

The fact that family firms have survived in the top industrialised countries, is surely due to a set of 'structural' internal factors which have enhanced their competitiveness and ability to react to market challenges. These 'competitive advantages' (which have been viewed as 'disadvantages' in literature adverse to family firms) include quick decision-making combined with long-term planning and commitment reinforced by a dividend policy directed toward the accumulation of capital (Yasuoka 1984b: 308ff.). These advantages are, however, the direct consequences of the reduction of internal transaction and agency costs, arising from the coincidence between the family and the firm. Another relevant explanation for the family firm's persistence lies in elements that are rooted in a particular context. In other words, it is important to take account of the country's system of values, culture, and ideology, all of which shape the institutional framework influencing the form – and consequently, the strengths and weaknesses – of a family firm.

Generally speaking, at a *micro* level and in a historical perspective, it is possible to identify two different behavioural patterns that can determine the success – or decline – of the family firm. On the one hand, there is the traditional model of the 'familialistic' or 'dynastic' firm (this definition is taken from Casson 2000). In this case the identification of the family with the firm is almost complete. The main goal is to preserve the enterprise, or, if possible, increase its success as an asset for the whole family. The enterprise is viewed as the main source of wealth and subsistence for family members who are expected to find a job in the firm itself. Even in the case of a complex organisation, the top management positions are assigned to family members, while the only chance for outsiders to achieve upward mobility is to enter the family itself via marriage strategies. The leadership succession process, even in the presence of advanced methods of selection and training, is in any case managed inside the family, with very limited recourse to consultants and professionals. As a consequence, 'dynastic' firms are rarely innovative, and tend to preserve the competitive advantage gained during the start-up period. It is possible that they can count on such an advantage in terms of market, product, or know-how and assume that this position will go unchallenged in the medium period. In another successful scenario, transaction and information costs are so high that maintaining every managerial responsibility inside the family is the only possible way to operate. One clear advantage of the dynastic firm is the strong commitment and long-term training of the family members – counterbalanced by the lesser motivation of middle management, who are prevented from reaching the top positions.

Another typology is that of the 'open family firm'. In this case, even if family control is unquestioned, a relevant issue is the presence of outsiders in key positions. Family members are not expected to enter the firm as a matter of course, but only after serious training, and the outsiders compete with insiders for top positions. In this instance, the risks involved in the hiring of non-family-members are counterbalanced by the necessity to break up the routines inherited from past generations. It is clear that this pattern is to be found where dynamism, in terms of rate of growth or market evolution, is high at the same time as transaction costs are low.

The historical perspective deployed in this study, emphasising the relationships of the family firms with their context, is consistent with a more dynamic consideration of the subject. Quoting Mark Casson, 'the family firm is neither an anachronism – as conventional neo-classical economics suggests – nor a viable replacement for the modern managerial corporation. It is, however, a valuable member of the set of institutional forms available to entrepreneurs within a market economy' (Casson 2000: 220–1). This study has provided an account of the shifting controversy surrounding the impact of family firms in modern and mature economies. It has also reaffirmed the need to place business in its social, historical, institutional, and economic context. It remains to be seen how far multidisciplinary approaches will move the analysis of family firms forward, always bearing in mind that business historians will continue to take seriously this particular organisational form in view of its survival and continuing proliferation.

Bibliographical essay

Family business is a very broad issue and the point of convergence of several research fields, from psychology, history, economics, anthropology, and other social sciences to management disciplines, consulting, and business administration. This means that it is almost impossible to provide a complete account within a short bibliographical essay of the large amount of research concerned with personal capitalism and family firms.

This short essay provides a synthesis of current debates on the topic. It also identifies the seminal works on the subject. Due to limitations of space the essay highlights broad and comparative research.

Overviews and sourcebooks

A useful introduction to the topic is the collection of papers published in the *International Library of Critical Writings in Business History*, no. 13 (Elgar Reference Collection, Aldershot, UK, and Brooksfield, USA, 1995), edited by Mary B. Rose. In collaboration with the same author, I have published a short essay, 'Family Firms in Comparative Perspective', in a volume edited by Franco Amatori and Geoffrey Jones entitled *Business History Around the World at the Turn of the Century* (Cambridge University Press, 2001). There we provide additional bibliographical information emphasising both cultural and institutional perspectives.

Another important collection of articles and papers is to be found in the volume edited by Craig Aronoff, Joseph Astrachan, and John Ward entitled *Family Business Sourcebook II* (Business Owner Resources, Marietta, Ga., 1996). The quarterly issues of the *Family*

Business Review, an international journal devoted to interdisciplinary research on the subject, provide an updated source of information.

Conferences and colloquia

The issue of family capitalism has been the subject of discussion at various conferences, seminars, and colloquia where the work of Alfred Chandler, emphasising the close relationship between large, managerial public companies and the 'wealth of the nation', has provided the focus of debate. Chandlerian scholars have explicitly connected the persistence of family firms and personal capitalism to a loss of competitive strength and to a general economic backwardness. Some comparative research has tried to explore the different national patterns of managerial capitalism together with the resistance posed by 'old' organisational patterns. For instance, in 1982 at the Eleventh International Economic History Congress, Leslie Hannah organised the proceedings of the congress into a volume entitled *From Family Firm to Professional Management* (Akadémiai Kiadó, Budapest), encompassing several papers based on national and sectoral case studies. All the papers deal with the persistence and the role of family capitalism, and the volume provides a valuable analysis of the different national and historical patterns of the emergence of managerial enterprise. In this same work, Roy Church, writing on the motor industry ('The Transition from Family Firm to Managerial Enterprise in the Motor Industry: an International Comparison'), introduces a less deterministic perspective on the role of family firms in modern capitalism. He argues for the potential co-existence of different organisational models equally efficient in different markets and cultures. This suggestion was reaffirmed in 1984 at the Tenth International Fuji Conference, devoted to 'Family Business in the Era of Industrial Growth'. (The proceedings of the conference have been edited by Akio Okochi and Shigeaki Yasuoka, University of Tokyo Press.) It was the Japanese contributors especially who demonstrated that the successful economic growth of the country during the period between the two World Wars was perfectly consistent with the persistence and diffusion of large family-controlled concerns, the *zaibatsu*. Since the end of the 1980s a new stream of research has been increasingly critical of the paradigm of convergence toward managerial capitalism, considering it too deterministic, and inadequate as a satisfactory explanation of the dynamics of Western industrialisation. The emphasis on the historical, cultural, and institutional determinants of different national patterns of development is evident in some recent comparative research on European enterprises. In these cases the persistence of family capitalism inside a given national economic system is considered not as an inefficient deviation from the Chandlerian optimum, but on the contrary as the best organisational solution in a particular context. Family firms perform, it is shown, at the same level as their managerial counterparts.

The contributions by Patrick Fridenson (on France), Ulrich Wengenroth (on Germany), and Geoffrey Jones (on Great Britain), collected by Alfred Chandler, Franco Amatori, and Takashi Hikino in *Big Business and the Wealth of Nations* (Cambridge University Press, 1997), are probably the most complete and updated syntheses on the emergence of big business in the contemporary economies. Other instances of comparative research contain explicit critiques of the convergence paradigm, for instance Margarita Dritsas and Terry Gourvish (eds.), *European Enterprise: Strategies of Adaptation and Renewal in the Twentieth Century* (Trochalia Publications, Athens, 1997) and Margrit Müller (ed.), *Structure and Strategy of Small and Medium Size Enterprises since the Industrial Revolution*, Zeitschrift für Unternehmensgeschichte, Beiheft 83, Stuttgart 1994.

Much more explicit in this regard, *Family Capitalism* is a special issue of the British journal, *Business History*, 35 (1993), edited by Geoffrey Jones and Mary B. Rose, which contains several essays on the topic. Both the volume's introduction and a provocative essay by Church ('The Family Firm in Industrial Capitalism: International Perspectives on Hypotheses and History') point to the need for a new perspective emphasising national differences. Further suggestions in this direction come in Youssef Cassis's book, *Big Business. The European Experience in the 20th Century* (Oxford University Press, 1997), as well as from Tom McCraw (ed.), *Creating Modern Capitalism* (Harvard University Press, Cambridge, Mass., 1997), which, while not explicitly dealing with the issue of family capitalism, provides useful evidence on the subject. The role of small family firms in developed Western economies and Japan is one of the themes contained in the book edited by Konosuke Odaka and Minoru Saway (eds.), *Small Firms, Large Concerns. The Development of Small Business in Comparative Perspective* (Oxford University Press, 1999). This volume summarises the proceedings of the last Fuji Conference in Japan.

National cases

The above-mentioned research provides useful insights into new perspectives on the role of family capitalism in modern economic growth. It is worth adding, however, some further work on different area patterns. The British, for instance, have been particularly productive in the field of studies concerning the effective role of family firms during the first industrial revolution. For a summary and discussion, see W. D. Rubinstein, *Capitalism, Culture and Decline in Britain, 1750–1990* (Routledge, London and New York, 1993), which discusses and partially refutes the widespread thesis on the decline of British entrepreneurial spirit. Several such contributions have stressed the positive contribution of personal capitalism also in services and finance – see, for instance, Maurice Kirby and Mary B. Rose (eds.), *Business Enterprise in Modern Britain* (Routledge, London, 1994); Jonathan Brown and Mary B. Rose (eds.), *Entrepreneurship, Networks and Modern Business* (Manchester University Press, 1993); and finally John F. Wilson, *British Business History 1720–1994* (Manchester University Press, 1995). In the case of Germany, Jurgen Kocka's *Industrial Culture and Bourgeois Society: Business, Labor, and Bureaucracy in Modern Germany* (Berghahn Books, New York and London, 1999) sets out the contrasts between traditional, personal, and family capitalism in the emerging large industries of the second industrial revolution and managerial capitalism. On France, it is worth citing Dean Savage, *Founders, Heirs and Managers. French Industrial Leadership in Transition* (Sage, Beverly Hills, 1979). A historical perspective is given in the important essay by Patrick Fridenson in Chandler, Ameton and Hikino (eds.), *Big Business and the Wealth of Nations* and in two articles by Emmanuel Chadeau, 'The Large Family Firm in Twentieth-Century France' (in Jones and Rose, *Family Capitalism*) and 'Mass Retailing: a last chance for the family firm in France?' published in Youssef Cassis, François Crouzet, and Terry Gourvish (eds.),

Management and Business in Britain and France. The Age of the Corporate Economy (Clarendon Press, Oxford, 1995). Further evidence on the French experience is contained in two issues of the French review *Entreprises et Histoire* (9 (1995) and 12 (1996)) dealing with the topic 'Entrepreneurial Dynasties'.

Even if the economic development of the main Mediterranean countries has been largely dominated by family firms, it is difficult to find major research available on this subject, at least in English. In the case of Italy, for instance, the family firm must be considered a permanent actor in the country's industrial history. When private big business is considered, researchers frequently stress the close relationship between the dominance of family capitalism at almost every level and the country's 'failed landing' after the sharp growth of the 1960s (see Franco Amatori, 'Italy: the Tormented Rise of Organizational Capabilities between Government and Families', in *Big Business and the Wealth of Nations*). On the other hand, where the highly dispersed and uncertain world of small business is concerned, the close identification between the family and the firm is perceived as an asset, granting both flexibility and stability (see, on this, Edward Goodman and Julia Bamford (eds.), *Small Firms and Industrial Districts in Italy* (Routledge, London, 1989)). More recently and from a historical point of view, Aurelio Alaimo follows the argument in his 'Small Manufacturing Firms and Local Productive Systems in Modern Italy', in Konosuke Odaka and Minoru Saway (eds.), *Small Firms, Large Concerns*. I discuss the role of networks of small and medium-sized family firms in my 'Networking the Market. Evidence and Conjectures from the History of the Italian Industrial Districts', *European Yearbook of Business History*, 1 (1998).

Given the strict connection between the organisational and ownership structure of an enterprise and the institutional and cultural morphology of the country, the Japanese (especially in the period preceding the Second World War) and Far Eastern cases are particularly significant. On Japan, it is worth highlighting the studies by Hidemasa Morikawa on *zaibatsu* – *Zaibatsu. The Rise and Fall of Family Enterprise Groups in Japan* (University of Tokyo Press, 1992), and the very recent *A History of Top Management in Japan. Managerial Enterprises and Family Enterprises* (Oxford University Press, 2001) – as well as another useful article by Haruito Takeda,

'Japanese Zaibatsu Revisited', *Entreprises et Histoire*, 21 (June, 1999), pp. 90–9. On the Far East and China, see Gary G. Hamilton (ed.), *Asian Business Networks* (De Gruyter, Berlin, 1996), and Mark Fruin (ed.), *Networks, Markets and the Pacific Rim. Studies in Strategy* (Oxford University Press, New York and Oxford, 1998). On the role of family-owned conglomerates in underdeveloped economies, see a special issue of the journal *The Developing Economies* (21 (4), December 1993) entitled *Business Groups in Developing Economies* – comparing the cases of Thailand, Indonesia, the Philippines, Korea, Taiwan, and Mexico – but above all the book by Alice Amsden, *The Rise of 'the Rest': Challenges to the West from Late-Industrialising Economies* (Oxford University Press, 2001).

Historical alternatives

Another promising field of research is that of the so-called 'historical alternatives to mass production'. In these cases the family firm is considered one of the main building blocks in industrialisation. This perspective mostly draws upon the ability of small and medium producers to build up networks of firms able to fulfil the needs of rapidly changing demand, for instance in the case of the fashion industry or in that of specialised producers. Family firms are in this perspective essential in providing a rapid response to market changes on the basis of their high information and trust and hence low transaction costs. In this setting, a substantial contribution comes from the research of Philip Scranton on specialised production and proprietary capitalism in the American economy – *Proprietary Capitalism. The Textile Manufacture in Philadelphia 1880–1885* (Cambridge University Press, 1983); *Figured Tapestry. Production, Markets and Power in Philadelphia Textile 1885–1941* (Cambridge University Press, 1989); and the recent *Endless Novelty. Speciality Production and American Industrialisation (1865–1925)* (Princeton University Press, 1997), especially the introduction by the author. In the same class are the famous works by Michael Piore and Charles Sabel, *The Second Industrial Divide* (Basic Books, New York, 1984); Sabel and Jonathan Zeitlin, 'Historical Alternatives to Mass Production: Politics, Markets and Technology in Nineteenth-Century Industrialisation', *Past and Present*, 108 (1985); and a recent book edited by Sabel and Zeitlin, *World of Possibilities: Flexibility and Mass Production in Western*

Industrialisation (Cambridge University Press, 1997). A synthesis of this approach is provided by Zeitlin in the chapter entitled 'Productive Alternatives: Flexibility, Governance, and Strategic Choice in Industrial History', in F. Amatori and G. Jones (eds.), *Business History Around the World*.

Theory and current debates

The family firm has been traditionally considered a privileged field of research for testing the assumptions of the transaction cost theory. From another perspective, the study of the role and performance of the family firm in a particular national context helps to relativise the concept of organisational efficiency, taking into account the influence of different historical, institutional, and cultural settings.

On the first point, a relevant contribution is by Mats Alvesson and Lars Lindkvist, 'Transaction Costs, Clans and Corporate Culture', *Journal of Management Studies*, 30 (3) (1993), pp. 427–52, as well as the classic paper by Yoram Ben-Porath, 'The F-Connection: Families, Friends and Firms and the Organisation of Exchange', *Population Development Review*, 6 (1) (1980), and Robert Pollak, 'A Transaction Cost Approach to Families and Households', *Journal of Economic Literature*, 33 (1985), pp. 581–608. For a broader theoretical approach, see Mark Casson, *Enterprise and Leadership* (Elgar, Cheltenham, and Northampton, Mass., 2000), especially ch. 8, 'The Family Firm: an Analysis of the Dynastic Motive'.

During the last few years some new issues and debates have arisen, the most relevant of which can be summarised as follows:

a. the effective role and relevance of family firms, especially those of larger size, inside a national economy;
b. the issues of leadership and leadership succession as crucial to the firm's survival. This field is widely analysed, above all by economists and consultants (see, for instance, Ivan Lansberg, *Succeeding Generations* (Harvard Business School Press, Boston, Mass., 1999), and Fred Neubauer and Alden G. Lank, *The Family Business: its Governance for Sustainability* (Routledge, New York, 1998);
c. the issues of corporate governance involving especially fast-growing family firms that are more and more counting on

external finance to sustain their expansion but are at the same time unwilling to transform their ownership structures. Although this is not a negligible phenomenon in modern advanced economies, it is not easy to find comparative evidence of the impact on major family firms of the new regulation policies in the capital markets. Information on this topic can be found, if not systematically, in Richard Whittington and Michael Mayer, *The European Corporation. Strategy, Structure and Social Science* (Oxford University Press, 2000), particularly chapters 4 and 7, and in the recent Fabrizio Barca and Marco Becht (eds.), *The Control of Corporate Europe* (Oxford University Press, 2001).

Bibliography

Alaimo, Aurelio, 'Small Manufacturing Firms and Local Productive Systems in Modern Italy', in Konosuke Odaka and Minoru Saway (eds.), *Small Firms, Large Concerns*, Oxford University Press, 1999

Albert, Michel, 1991, *Capitalisme contre Capitalisme*, Editions du Seuil, Paris

Alcorn, P. B., 1982, *Success and Survival in the Family Owned Business*, McGraw Hill, New York, 1982

Alvesson, Mats and Lindkvist, Lars, 1993, 'Transaction Costs, Clans and Corporate Culture', *Journal of Management Studies*, 30 (3), pp. 427–52

Amatori, Franco, 1989, *Proprietà e direzione. La Rinascente, 1917–1969*, Angeli, Milan

  1996, *Impresa e mercato. Lancia 1906–1969*, Il Mulino, Bologna

  1997a, 'Italy: The Tormented Rise of Organisational capabilities between government and families', in Chandler, Amatori, and Hikino 1997, ch. 8

  1997b, 'Growth via Politics. Business Groups Italian Style', in Shiba and Shimotani 1997, pp. 19–134

Amatori, Franco and Colli, Andrea, 2000, *Impresa e industria in Italia dall'Unità ad oggi*, Marsilio, Venice

Ampalavanar Brown, Rajeswary, ed., 1995, *Chinese Business Enterprise in Asia*, Routledge, London

Amsden, Alice H., 1997, 'South Korea: Enterprising Groups and Entrepreneurial Government', in Chandler, Amatori, and Hikino 1997, pp. 336–67

  2001, *The Rise of 'the Rest'. Challenges to the West from Late-industrialising Economies*, Oxford University Press, 2001

Amsden, Alice H. and Hikino, Takashi, 1994, 'Staying Behind, Stumbling Back, Sneaking Up, Soaring Ahead: Late Industrialisation in Historical Perspective', in W. Baumol, R. Nelson, and E. Wolff (eds.), *Convergence of Productivity: Cross-Country Studies and Historical Evidence*, Oxford University Press, New York

Arnoldus, Doreen J. G., 2002, *Family, Family Firm and Strategy. Six Dutch Family Firms in the Food Industry, 1880–1970*, NEHA, Amsterdam

Aronoff, Craig E., Astrachan, Joseph H. and Ward, John L., eds., 1996, *Family Business Sourcebook II*, Business Owner Resources, Marietta, Ga.

Ayres, Glenn R., 1990, 'Rough Justice: Equity in Family Business Succession Planning', *Family Business Review*, 3, pp. 3–22

Bairati, Piero, 1988, *Le dinastie imprenditoriali*, in Melograni 1988, pp. 141–92

Banfield, Edward C., 1958, *The Moral Basis of a Backward Society*, The Free Press Corp., New York

Barca, Fabrizio and Becht, Marco, eds., 2001, *The Control of Corporate Europe*, Oxford University Press

Barca, Fabrizio, Iwai, Katsuhito, Pagano, Ugo and Trento, Sandro, 1998, *Post-War Institutional Shocks. The Divergence of Italian and Japanese Corporate Governance Models*, special issue of *Quaderni del Dipartimento di Economia Politica dell'Università degli Studi di Siena* (234)

Barca, F., Bianchi, M., Brioschi, F., Buzzacchi, L., Casavola, P., Filippa, L. and Pagnini, M., 1994, *Assetti proprietari e mercato delle imprese. Vol. II. Gruppo. Proprietà e controllo nelle imprese italiane medio-grandi*, Il Mulino, Bologna

Barker, Thomas C., 1977, *The Glassmakers. Pilkington: The Rise of an International Company, 1926–1976*, Weidenfeld and Nicolson, London

Barker, Thomas C. and Lévy-Leboyer, Maurice, 1982, 'An Inquiry into the Buddenbrooks Effect in Europe', in Hannah 1982, pp. 10–25

Barnes, Louis B., and Hershon, Simon A., 1976, 'Transferring Power in the Family Business', *Harvard Business Review*, July–August, pp. 105–14

Barry, Bernard, 1975, 'The Development of Organisation Structure in the Family Firm', *Journal of General Management*, 3 (1), pp. 42–60

Becht, Marco, 1997, *Strong Blockholders, Weak Owners and the Need for European Mandatory Disclosure*, ECGN paper

Ben-Porath, Yoram, 1980, 'The F-Connection: Families, Friends and Firms and the Organisation of Exchange', *Population Development Review*, 6 (1), pp. 1–30, also reprinted in Rose 1995a: pp. 179–208

Berle, Adolf, and Means, Gardiner C., 1932, *The Modern Corporation and Private Property*, Macmillan, New York

Bernstein, Jeffrey R., 1997, 'Japanese Capitalism', in T. McCraw (ed.), *Creating Modern Capitalism*, Harvard University Press, Cambridge, Mass., and London, pp. 439–89

Bianchi, M., Bianco, M. and Enriques, L., 2001, *Pyramidal Groups and the Separation Between Ownership and Control in Italy*, in Barca and Becht 2001, ch. 6

Bianco, Magda and Casavola, Paola, 1996, 'Corporate Governance in Italia: alcuni fatti e problemi aperti', in *Rivista delle Società*, pp. 426–39

Brioschi, Francesco, Buzzacchi, Luigi and Colombo, Massimo G., 1990, *Gruppi di imprese e mercato finanziario. La struttura di potere nell'industria italiana*, Nuova Italia Scientifica, Rome

Brockstedt, Jürgen, 1984, 'Family Enterprise and the Rise of Large-Scale Enterprise in Germany (1871–1914) – Ownership and Management', in Okochi and Yasuoka 1984, pp. 237–67

Brown, Jonathan, and Rose, Mary B., eds., 1993, *Entrepreneurship, Networks and Modern Business*, Manchester University Press

Burch, Philip H., Jr, 1972, *The Managerial Revolution Reassessed. Family Control in America's Large Corporations*, D. C. Heath & Co., Lexington

Cassis, Youssef, 1994, *City Bankers, 1890–1914*, Cambridge University Press

1995, 'Divergence and Convergence in British and French Business in the Nineteenth and Twentieth Centuries', in Cassis, Crouzet, and Gourvish 1995, pp. 1–30

1997, *Big Business. The European Experience in the Twentieth Century*, Oxford University Press

Cassis, Youssef, Crouzet, François and Gourvish, Terry, eds., 1995, *Management and Business in Britain and France. The Age of the Corporate Economy*, Clarendon Press, Oxford

Casson, Mark, 1993, 'Entrepreneurship and Business Culture', in Brown and Rose 1993

2000, *Enterprise and Leadership. Studies on Firms, Markets and Networks*, Elgar, Cheltenham and Northampton, Mass.

Castronovo, Valerio, 1999, *Fiat 1899–1999. Un secolo di storia italiana*, RCS Libri, Milan

Chadeau, Emmanuel, 1993, 'The Large Family Firm in Twentieth-Century France', in Jones and Rose 1993, pp. 184–205

1995, 'Mass Retailing: A Last Chance for the Family Firm in France?' in Cassis, Crouzet, and Gourvish 1995, pp. 52–71

Chalmers, Ian and Hadiz, Vedi R., eds., 1997, *The Politics of Economic Development in Indonesia*, Routledge, London

Chandler, Alfred D., Jr, 1962, *Strategy and Structure*, MIT Press, Cambridge, Mass.

1980, 'The United States. Seedbed of Managerial Capitalism', in Chandler and Daems 1980, pp. 9–40

1990a, *Scale and Scope. The Dynamics of Industrial Capitalism*, Harvard University Press, Cambridge, Mass., and London

1990b, 'The Enduring Logic of Industrial Success', *Harvard Business Review*, 2, pp. 130–40

1994, 'The Competitive Performance of US Industrial Enterprises since the Second World War', *Business History Review*, 68, Spring, pp. 1–72

1997, 'The United States: Engines of Economic Growth in the Capital-intensive and Knowledge-intensive Industries', in Chandler, Amatori, and Hikino 1997, pp. 63–101

Chandler, Alfred D., Jr, and Daems, Herman, eds., 1980, *Managerial Hierarchies. Comparative Perspectives on the Rise of the Modern Industrial Enterprise*, Harvard University Press, Cambridge, Mass.

Chandler, Alfred D., Jr, and Hikino, Takashi, 1997, 'The large industrial enterprise and the dynamics of economic growth', in Chandler, Amatori, and Hikino 1997, pp. 24–62

Chandler, Alfred D., Jr, Amatori, Franco and Hikino, Takashi, eds., 1997, *Big Business and the Wealth of Nations*, Cambridge University Press, New York

Chapman, Stanley, 1984, *The Rise of Merchant Banking*, Allen & Unwin, London

Chen, Min, 1995, *Asian Management Systems. Chinese, Japanese and Korean Styles of Business*, Routledge, London

Chiesi, Antonio, 1986, 'Fattori di persistenza del capitalismo familiare', *Stato e Mercato*, 18, pp. 433–53

Church, Roy, 1982, 'The Transition from Family Firm to Managerial Enterprise in the Motor Industry: An International Comparison', in Hannah 1982, pp. 26–38

1993, 'The Family Firm in Industrial Capitalism: International Perspectives on Hypotheses and History', in Jones and Rose 1993, pp. 17–43

Colli, Andrea, 1998, 'Networking the Market. Evidence and Conjectures from the History of the Italian Industrial Districts', *European Yearbook of Business History*, 1, pp. 75–92

Colli, Andrea and Rose, Mary B., 1999, *Families and Firms: The Culture and Evolution of Family Firms in Britain and Italy in the Nineteenth and Twentieth Centuries*, Scandinavian Economic History Review, 47 (1)

2002, 'Family Firms in Comparative Perspective', in F. Amatori and G. Jones (eds.), *Business History Around the World at the Turn of the Century*, Cambridge University Press, Cambridge and New York

Colli, Andrea, Pérez, Paloma Fernandez and Rose, Mary B., 2001, 'Family Firms and Leadership Succession in Europe during the Nineteenth and Twentieth centuries. The Case of Britain, Italy and Spain', unpublished paper, August 2000

Corbetta, Guido, 1995, *Le imprese familiari. Caratteri originali, varietà e condizioni di sviluppo*, Egea, Milan

2001, 'Family Business', in Neil J. Smelser and Paul B. Baltes, eds., *International Encyclopaedia of the Social and Behavioural Sciences*, Pergamon Press, Oxford

Corbetta, Guido and Montemerlo, Daniela, 1999, 'Ownership, Governance and Management Issues in Small and Medium Size Family

Businesses: A Comparison of Italy and the United States', *Family Business Review*, 12 (4), pp. 361–74

Corbetta, Guido and Tomaselli, Salvo, 1996, 'Boards of Directors in Italian Family Businesses', *Family Business Review*, 9 (4), pp. 403–21

Cossentino, Francesco, Pyke, Frank and Segemberger, Werner, 1996, *Local and Regional Responses to Global Pressure: The Case of Italy and its Industrial Districts*, International Labour Organisation, Geneva

Daems, H., 1980, 'The Rise of the Modern Industrial Enterprise: A New Perspective', in Chandler and Daems 1980, pp. 203–23

Davenport, Richard P. T. and Jones, G., eds., 1988, *Enterprise, Management and Innovation in British Business 1914–1980*, Cass, London

De Ferrière le Vayer, Marc, 1995, 'Christofle: A Family Firm', in Cassis, Crouzet, and Gourvish 1995, pp. 72–87

De Roover, Raymond, 1963, *The Rise and Decline of the Medici Bank, 1397–1494*, Harvard University Press, Cambridge, Mass.

Dei Ottati, Gabi, 1994, 'Trust, Interlinking Transactions and Credit in the Industrial District', *Cambridge Journal of Economics*, December, 529–46

Dobkin Hall, Peter, 1988, 'A Historical Overview of Family Firms in the United States', *Family Business Review*, 1 (1)

Donckels, R. and Frohlich, E., 1991, *Are Family Businesses really different? European Experiences from STRATOS*, *Family Business Review*, 2

Donnelley, Robert G., 1964, 'The Family Business', *Harvard Business Review*, 42 (4), July–August, pp. 93–105

Dore, Ronald, 2000, *Stock Market Capitalism: Welfare Capitalism. Japan and Germany versus the Anglo-Saxons*, Oxford University Press

Dritsas, Margarita, 1997, 'Family Firms in Greek Industry During the Twentieth Century', in Dritsas and Gourvish 1997, pp. 85–103

Dritsas, Margarita and Gourvish, Terry, eds., 1997, *European Enterprise: Strategies of Adaptation and Renewal in the Twentieth Century*, Trochalia, Athens

Dutta, Sudipt, 1996, *Family Business in India*, Sage Publications, New Delhi

Dyer, W. G., Jr, 1986, *Cultural Change in Family Firms. Anticipating and Managing Business and Family Transition*, Jossey-Bass Publishers, San Francisco and London

Dyer, W. G., Jr, and Sanchez, M., 1998, 'Current State of Family Business Theory and Practice as Reflected in Family Business Review 1988–1997', *Family Business Review*, 4 (11), pp. 287–95

Elbaum, Bernard and Lazonick, William, 1986, *The Decline of the British Economy*, Clarendon Press, Oxford

Fear, Jeffrey, 1997, 'August Thyssen and German Steel', in T. McCraw (ed.), *Creating Modern Capitalism*, Harvard University Press, Cambridge, Mass., ch. 6

Fitzgerald, Robert, 1995, 'Ownership, Organisation and Management: British Business and the Branded Consumer Good Industry', in Cassis, Crouzet, and Gourvish 1995, pp. 31–51

Fridenson, Patrick, 1997, 'France: The Relatively Slow Development of Big Business in the Twentieth Century', in Chandler, Amatori, and Hikino 1997, pp. 207–45

Fruin, Mark, ed., 1998, *Networks, Markets and the Pacific Rim. Studies in Strategy*, Oxford University Press, New York and Oxford

Galambos, Lou, 1983, 'Technology, Political Economy and Professionalization: Central Themes of the Organizational Synthesis', *Business History Review*, 57, pp. 471–93

Galbraith, John Kenneth, 1967, *The New Industrial State*, Houghton Mifflin Co., Boston

Gallo, Miguel A., 1995, 'Family Businesses in Spain: Tracks Followed and Outcomes Reached by those among the Largest Thousand', *Family Business Review*, 8 (4), pp. 245–54

Gallo, Miguel and Pont, G., 1988, 'The Family Business in the Spanish Economy', IESE research paper

Gennaro, Pietro, 1985, 'Le imprese familiari di grande dimensione in Italia', *Sviluppo e Organizzazione*, 87, Jan.–Feb., pp. 15–19

Gerschenkron, Alexander, 1962, *Economic Backwardness in Historical Perspective. A Book of Essays*, The Belknap Press of Harvard University Press, Cambridge, Mass.

Goodman, Edward and Bamford, Julia, eds., 1989, *Small Firms and Industrial Districts in Italy*, Routledge, London

Gourvish, Terry, 1988, 'British Business and the Transition to a Corporate Economy: Entrepreneurship and Management Structures', in Davenport and Jones 1988, pp. 18–64

Granovetter, Mark, 1996, 'Coase Revisited: Business Groups in the Modern Economy', *Industrial and Corporate Change*, 4, pp. 93–130

Hamilton, Gary G., ed., 1996, *Asian Business Networks*, De Gruyter, Berlin
    1998, 'Patterns of Asian Network Capitalism. The Cases of Taiwan and South Korea', in Fruin 1998, pp. 181–99

Hamilton, Gary G. and Feenstra, Robert C., 1996, 'Varieties of Hierarchies and Markets: An Introduction', *Industrial and Corporate Change*, 4, pp. 51–91

Hannah, Leslie, 1980, 'Visible and Invisible Hands in Great Britain', in Chandler and Daems 1980, pp. 41–76
    ed., 1982, *From Family Firm to Professional Management: Structure and Performance of Business Enterprise*, Akadémiai Kiadó, Budapest
    1983, *The Rise of the Corporate Economy*, Methuen, London

Hau, Michel, 1995, 'Traditions comportamentales et capitalisme dynastique. Le cas des "grandes familles"', *Entreprises et Histoire*, 9, pp. 43–59

Hofstede, Geert, 1980, *Culture's Consequences. International Differences in Work-related Values*, Sage, London

Holl, P., 1975, 'Effect of Control Type on the Performance of the Firm in the UK', *Journal of Industrial Economics*, 23 (4), pp. 257–72

Jacquemin, Alexis and De Ghellinck, Elizabeth, 1980, 'Familial Control, Size and Performance in the Largest French Firms', *European Economic Review*, 13 (1), pp. 81–92

Jones, Geoffrey, 2000, *Merchants to Multinationals. British Trading Companies in the Nineteenth and Twentieth Centuries*, Oxford University Press

Jones, Geoffrey and Rose, Mary B., eds., 1993, *Family Capitalism*, Frank Cass, London (special issue of *Business History*: 35)

Kang, Chul-Kyu, 1997, 'Diversification Process and the Ownership Structure of Samsung Chaebol', in Shiba and Shimotani 1997, pp. 31–58

Kirby, Maurice, 1994, 'The Corporate Economy in Britain: Its Rise and Achievements since 1900', in Kirby and Rose 1994, ch. 6

Kirby, Maurice and Rose, Mary B., eds., 1994, *Business Enterprise in Modern Britain*, Routledge, London

Kocka, Jürgen, 1971, 'Family and Bureaucracy in German Industrial Management, 1850–1914. Siemens in Comparative Perspective', *Business History Review*, 45 (2), pp. 133–56

1999, *Industrial Culture and Bourgeois Society. Business, Labor, and Bureaucracy in Modern Germany*, Berghahn Books, New York and London

Koike, Kenji, ed., 1993, *Business Groups in Developing Economies*, special issue of *Developing Economies*: 31 (4)

Lamoreaux, Naomi R., 1994, *Insider Lending: Banks, Personal Connections and Economic Development in Industrial New England*, Cambridge University Press

Landes, David S., 1949, 'French Entrepreneurship and Industrial Growth in the Nineteenth Century', *Journal of Economic History*, 9 (1), pp. 45–61

1975, 'Bleichröders and Rothschilds', in Charles E. Rosenberg (ed.), *The Family in History*, University of Pennsylvania Press, Philadelphia

1976, 'Religion and Enterprise: The Case of the French Textile Industry', in Edward C. Carter, Robert Forster and Joseph N. Moody (eds.), *Enterprise and Entrepreneurs in Nineteenth and Twentieth-Century France*, Johns Hopkins University Press, Baltimore and London, pp. 41–86

Lane, Frederic C., 1944a, *Andrea Barbarigo, Merchant of Venice*, Johns Hopkins University Press, Baltimore

1944b, 'Family Partnerships and Joint Ventures', *Journal of Economic History*, 4, pp. 178–96

Langlois, Richard N. and Robertson, Paul L., 1995, *Firms, Markets and Economic Change: A Dynamic Theory of Business Institutions*, Routledge, London

Lansberg, Ivan, 1999, *Succeeding Generations*, Harvard Business School Press, Boston, Mass.

Lansberg, Ivan and Perrow, Edith, 1991, 'Understanding and Working with Leading Family Businesses in Latin America', *Family Business Review*, 4 (2), Summer

Larner, Robert, 1966, 'Ownership and Control in the 200 Largest Non-financial Corporations, 1929 and 1963', *American Economic Review*, 56 (3), pp. 777–87

    1970, *Management Control and the Large Corporation*, Dunellen, New York

Larsson, Mats, Lindgren, Håkan and Nyberg, Daniel, 2000, 'Entrepreneurship, Active Ownership and Succession Strategies: The Long-term Viability of the Swedish Bonnier and Wallenberg Family Business Groups', in P. Poutziouris (ed.), *Tradition or Entrepreneurship in the New Economy?* Proceedings of the 11th Annual World Conference of the Family Business Network, in London, Manchester University Press

Lee, Yeon-ho, 1997, *The State, Society and Big Business in South Korea*, Routledge, London

Leech, D. and Leahy, J., 1991, 'Ownership Structures, Control and the Performance of Large British Companies', *Economic Journal*, 101 (409), pp. 1418–37

Leff, Nathaniel H., 1978, 'Industrial Organisation and Entrepreneurship in the Developing Countries: the Economic Groups', *Economic Development and Cultural Change*, 26 (4), pp. 661–75, reprinted in Rose 1995a: pp. 497–511

Levine, Joshua, 1999, *The Rise and Fall of the House of Barneys*, William Morrow and Co., New York

Levinson, Harry, 1971, 'Conflicts that Plague the Family Business', *Harvard Business Review*, March–April, pp. 90–5

Lévy-Leboyer, Maurice, 1984, 'The Large Family Firm in the French Manufacturing Industry', in Okochi and Yasuoka 1984, pp. 209–33

Lhermie, Christian, 2001, *Carrefour ou l'invention de l'hypermarché*, Vuibert, Paris

Lisle-Williams, Michael, 1984, 'Beyond the Market: The Survival of Family Capitalism in the English Merchant Banks', *British Journal of Sociology*, 35 (2), pp. 241–71

Livesay, Harold C., 1977, 'Entrepreneurial Persistence Through the Bureaucratic Age', *Business History Review*, 51 (4), pp. 415–43

Lodge, George C., and Vogel, Ezra F., eds., 1987, *Ideology and National Competitiveness*, Harvard Business School Press, Harvard

Mantle, Jonathan, 1999, *Benetton*, Sperling & Kupfer, Milan

Marris, Robert, 1964, *The Economic Theory of 'Managerial Capitalism'*, Macmillan, London

McCraw, Thomas K. and Tedlow, Richard S., 1997, 'Henry Ford, Alfred Sloan and the Three Phases of Marketing', in T. McCraw (ed.), *Creating Modern Capitalism*, Harvard University Press, Cambridge, Mass., ch. 8

McGivern, Chris, 1978, 'The Dynamics of Management Succession', *Management Decision* (1), pp. 32–46

Melograni, Piero, ed., 1988, *La famiglia italiana dall'Ottocento ad oggi*, Laterza, Bari

Miller, Michael B., 1981, *The Bon Marché. Bourgeois Culture and the Department Store, 1869–1920*, Allen & Unwin, London

Miyamoto, Matao, 1984, 'The Position and Role of Family Business in the Development of the Japanese Company System', in Okochi and Yasuoka 1984, pp. 39–91

Moine, Jean-Marie, 1989, *Les Barons du fer. Les maîtres de forges en Lorraine du milieu du 19e siècle aux années trente. Histoire sociale d'un patronat sidérurgique*, Presses Universitaires de Nancy

Monsen, Joseph, 1996, 'Ownership and Management: The Effect of Separation on Performance', in Aronoff, Astrachan, and Ward 1996, pp. 26–34

Monsen, R. J., Chiu, J. S. and Cooley, D. E., 1968, 'The Effect of the Separation of Ownership and Control on the Performance of the Large Firm', *Quarterly Journal of Economics*, 82 (3), pp. 435–51

Montemerlo, Daniela, 2001, *Il governo delle imprese familiari*, Egea, Milan

Morikawa, Hidemasa, 1992, *Zaibatsu. The Rise and Fall of Family Enterprise Groups in Japan*, University of Tokyo

1997, 'Japan: Increasing Organisational Capabilities of Large Industrial Enterprises, 1880s–1980s', in Chandler, Amatori, and Hikino 1997, pp. 307–35

2001, *A History of Top Management in Japan. Managerial Enterprises and Family Enterprises*, Oxford University Press

Müller, Margrit, 1996, 'Good Luck or Good Management? Multigenerational Family Control in Two Swiss Enterprises since the 19th Century', *Entreprises et Histoire*, 12, pp. 19–47

Nelson, Richard R., 1994, 'Evolutionary Theorising about Economic Change', in Smelser and Swedberg 1994, pp. 108–36

Neubauer, Fred and Lank, Alden G. 1998, *The Family Business: Its Governance for Sustainability*, Routledge, New York

North, Douglass C., 1990, *Institutions, Institutional Change and Economic Performance*, Cambridge University Press, New York

Okochi, Akio and Yasuoka, Shigeaki, eds., 1984, *Family Business in the Era of Industrial Growth. Its Ownership and Management*, University of Tokyo Press

Pavan, Robert J., 1973, *Strategy and Structure of the Italian Enterprise*, University Microfilms, Ann Arbor, Mich.

Payne, P. L., 1984, *Family Business in Britain: An Historical and Analytical Survey*, in Okochi and Yasuoka 1984, pp. 171–206

Penrose, Edith, 1959, *The Theory of the Growth of the Firm*, Oxford University Press

Pérez, Paloma Fernandez, 1997, *Family Firms in Modern Spain: Managing Survival, Leadership and Succession*, Universitat Pompeu Fabra, Working Paper

1999, 'Challenging the Loss of an Empire: González & Byass of Jerez', *Business History*, 41 (4), pp. 72–87

2000, 'Leadership Succession in Spanish Family Firms, Nineteenth to Twentieth Centuries', in A.-M. Kuijlaars, K. Prudon, and J. Visser (eds.), *Business and Society*, Centre of Business History, Rotterdam, pp. 503–11

Piore, Michael J. and Sabel, Charles F., 1984, *The Second Industrial Divide. Possibilities for Prosperity*, Basic Books, New York

Pollak, Robert A., 1985, 'A Transaction Cost Approach to Families and Households', *Journal of Economic Literature*, 33, pp. 581–608

Pollard, Sidney, 1981, *Peaceful Conquest. The Industrialisation of Europe 1760–1970*, Oxford University Press

Porter, Glenn, 1993, *The Rise of Big Business 1860–1920*, 2nd edition, Harlan Davidson, Wheeling, Ill

Redding, Gordon S., 1990, *The Spirit of Chinese Capitalism*, De Gruyter, Berlin and New York

Robinson, Richard, 1986, *Indonesia. The Rise of Capital*, Allen & Unwin, London

Rose, Mary B., 1993, 'Beyond Buddenbrooks: The Family Firm and the Management of Succession in Nineteenth Century Britain', in Brown and Rose 1993, pp. 127–43.

1994, 'The Family Firm in British Business 1780–1914', in Kirby and Rose 1994, pp. 61–87

ed., 1995a, *Family Business*, Elgar, Aldershot

1995b, 'Introduction', in Rose 1995a, pp. xiii–xxvi

1998, 'Networks and Leadership Succession in British Business in the 1950s', *German Yearbook of Business History*, 1, pp. 57–74

1999, 'Networks, Values and Business: The Evolution of British Family Firms from the Eighteenth to the Twentieth Century', *Entreprises et Histoire*, 22, pp. 16–30

2000, *Firms, Networks and Business Values: The British and American Cotton Industries since 1750*, Cambridge University Press

2001, 'Entrepreneurial Legacies and Leadership Succession in British Business in the 1950s', in S. Yonekura and M. J. Lynskey (eds.), *The Entrepreneur and Organisation: Comparative Perspectives*, Oxford University Press, Oxford

Rubinstein, W. D., 1993, *Capitalism, Culture and Decline in Britain, 1750–1990*, Routledge, London and New York

Sabel, Charles and Zeitlin, Jonathan, 1985, 'Historical Alternatives to Mass Production: Politics, Markets and Technology in Nineteenth-Century Industrialisation', *Past and Present*, 108, pp. 133–76

1997, *World of Possibilities: Flexibility and Mass Production in Western Industrialisation*, Cambridge University Press

Sargant Florence, P., 1961, *Ownership, Control and Success of Large Companies*, Sweet & Maxwell, London

Sato, Yuri, 1993, 'The Salim Group in Indonesia. The Development and Behaviour of the Largest Conglomerate in Southeast Asia', *Developing Economies*, 31 (4), pp. 408–41

Savage, Dean, 1979, *Founders, Heirs and Managers. French Industrial Leadership in Transition*, Sage, Beverly Hills

Schmitz, Christopher J., 1993, *The Growth of Big Business in the United States and Western Europe 1850–1939*, Cambridge University Press

Schröter, Harm, 1997, 'Small European Nations: Co-operative Capitalism in the Twentieth Century', in Chandler, Amatori, and Hikino 1997, pp. 176–204

Schumacher, Ernst F., 1973, *Small is Beautiful. A Study of Economics as if People Mattered*, Blond & Briggs Ltd, London

Scranton, Philip, 1983, *Proprietary Capitalism. The Textile Manufacture in Philadelphia 1880–1885*, Cambridge University Press

1986, 'Learning Manufacture: Shop Floor Schooling and the Family Firm', *Technology and Culture*, 27 (1), pp. 40–62

1989, *Figured Tapestry. Production, Markets and Power in Philadelphia Textile 1885–1941*, Cambridge University Press

1993, 'Build a Firm, Start Another: The Bromleys and Family Firm Entrepreneurship in the Philadelphia Region', *Business History*, 35 (4), pp. 115–41

1997, *Endless Novelty. Speciality Production and American Industrialisation, 1865–1925*, Princeton University Press

Shanker, Melissa C. and Astrachan, Joseph H., 1996, 'Myths and Realities: Family Businesses' Contribution to the US Economy – A Framework for Assessing Family Business Statistics', *Family Business Review*, 9 (2), pp. 107–24

Sheehan, Robert, 1967, 'Proprietors in the World of Big Business', *Fortune*, 15 June, pp. 168–84

Shiba, Takeo and Shimotani, Masahiro, eds., 1997, *Beyond the Firm. Business Groups in International and Historical Perspective*, Oxford University Press

Sluyterman, Keetie E., 1997, 'Three Centuries of De Kuyper: The Strength and Weakness of a Family Firm', in Dritsas and Gourvish 1997, pp. 105–22

Sluyterman, Keetie E. and Winkelman, Helene, 1993, 'The Dutch Family Firm Confronted with Chandler's Dynamics of Industrial Capitalism 1890–1940', in Jones and Rose 1993, pp. 152–83

Smelser, Neil J. and Swedberg, R., 1994, *The Handbook of Economic Sociology*, Princeton University Press

Stiefel, Dieter, 1997, 'The Rise and Fall of the House of Schenker: The Corporate Culture of Schenker Forwarding Company in the Three Generations of Family Ownership 1872–1931', in Dritsas and Gourvish 1997, pp. 161–73

Strachan, Harry W., 1976, *Family and other Business Groups in Economic Development; The Case of Nicaragua*, New York, Praeger

Suzuki, Kunio, 1997, 'From Zaibatsu to Corporate Complexes', in Shiba and Shimotani 1997, pp. 59–87

Takeda, Haruito, 1999, 'Japanese Zaibatsu Revisited', *Entreprises et Histoire*, 21, June, pp. 90–9

Thurow, Lester C., 1992, *Head to Head: Coming Economic Battle Among Japan, Europe and America*, Morrow, New York

Ungari, Paolo, 1974, *Profilo storico del diritto delle anonime in Italia*, Bulzoni, Rome

Verley, Patrick, 1997, *L'échelle du monde. Essai sur l'industrialisation de l'Occident*, Gallimard, Paris

Ward, John L., 1986, *Keeping the Family Business Healthy. How to Plan for Continuing Growth, Profitability and Family Leadership*, Jossey Bass, New York

    1992, *Creating Effective Boards for Private Enterprises: Meeting the Challenges of Continuity and Competition*, Jossey Bass, San Francisco

Ward, John L. and Aronoff, Craig E., 1996, 'Just What Is A Family Business?' in Aronoff, Astrachan, and Ward 1996, pp. 2–3

Whittington, Richard and Mayer, Michael, 2000, *The European Corporation. Strategy, Structure and Social Science*, Oxford University Press

Wiener, M. J., 1981, *English Culture and the Decline of Industrial Spirit*, Cambridge University Press

Williamson, O. E., 1981, 'The Modern Corporation: Origins, Evolution, Attributes', *Journal of Economic Literature*, 19, pp. 1537–68

Wilson, John F., 1995, *British Business History 1720–1994*, Manchester University Press

Wong, Siu-lun, 1985, 'The Chinese Family Firm: A Model', *British Journal of Sociology*, 36 (1), pp. 58–72, reprinted in Rose 1995a, pp. 621–35

Yamamura, Kozo, 1978, 'Entrepreneurship, Ownership and Management in Japan', in P. Mathias and M. M. Postan (eds.), *The Industrial Economies. Capital, Labour and Enterprise*, part 2, *The United States, Japan and Russia*, vol. VII of *The Cambridge Economic History of Europe*, Cambridge University Press, pp. 215–64

Yasuoka, Shigeaki, 1984a, 'Capital Ownership in Family Companies: Japanese Firms Compared with Those in Other Countries', in Okochi and Yasuoka 1984, pp. 1–32

1984b, 'Summary of the Concluding Discussion', in Okochi and Yasuoka 1984, pp. 305–14

1984c, 'The Tradition of Family Business in the Strategic Decision Process and Management Structure of Zaibatsu Business: Matsui, Sumitomo and Mitsubishi', in Keiichiro Nagakawa (ed.), *Strategy and Structure of Big Business*, Proceedings of the First Fuji Conference, University of Tokyo Press, pp. 81–101

Index

New Studies in Economic and Social History

Titles in the series available from Cambridge University Press

1 M. Anderson,
   Approaches to the History of the Western Family, 1500–1914
   ISBN 0 521 55260 5 (hardback) 0 521 55793 3 (paperback)

2 W. Macpherson,
   The Economic Development of Japan, 1868–1941
   ISBN 0 521 55792 5 (hardback) 0 521 55261 3 (paperback)

3 R. Porter,
   Disease, Medicine, and Society in England (second edition)
   ISBN 0 521 55262 1 (hardback) 0 521 55791 7 (paperback)

4 B. W. E. Alford,
   British Economic Performance since 1945
   ISBN 0 521 55263 X (hardback) 0 521 55790 9 (paperback)

5 A. Crowther,
   Social Policy in Britain, 1914–1939
   ISBN 0 521 55264 8 (hardback) 0 521 55789 5 (paperback)

6 E. Roberts,
   Women's Work, 1840–1940
   ISBN 0 521 55265 6 (hardback) 0 521 55788 7 (paperback)

7 C. Ó Grada,
   The Great Irish Famine
   ISBN 0 521 55266 4 (hardback) 0 521 55787 9 (paperback)

8 R. Rodger,
   Housing in Urban Britain, 1780–1914
   ISBN 0 521 55267 2 (hardback) 0 521 55786 0 (paperback)

ISBN 0 521 55280 X (hardback) 0 521 55773 9 (paperback)

22 J. Harrison,
    The Spanish Economy
    ISBN 0 521 55281 8 (hardback) 0 521 55772 0 (paperback)

23 C. Schmitz,
    *The Growth of Big Business in the United States and Western
    Europe, 1850–1939*
    ISBN 0 521 55282 6 (hardback) 0 521 55771 2 (paperback)

24 R. A. Church,
    The Rise and Decline of the British Motor Industry
    ISBN 0 521 55283 4 (hardback) 0 521 55770 4 (paperback)

25 P. Horn,
    Children's Work and Welfare, 1780–1880
    ISBN 0 521 55284 2 (hardback) 0 521 55769 0 (paperback)

26 R. Perren,
    Agriculture in Depression, 1870–1940
    ISBN 0 521 55285 0 (hardback) 0 521 55768 2 (paperback)

27 R. J. Overy,
    The Nazi Economic Recovery, 1932–1938 (second edition)
    ISBN 0 521 55286 9 (hardback) 0 521 55767 4 (paperback)

28 S. Cherry,
    Medical Services and the Hospitals in Britain, 1860–1939
    ISBN 0 521 57126 X (hardback) 0 521 57784 5 (paperback)

29 D. Edgerton,
    *Science, Technology and the British Industrial 'Decline',
    1870–1970*
    ISBN 0 521 57127 8 (hardback) 0 521 57778 0 (paperback)

30 C. A. Whatley,
    The Industrial Revolution in Scotland
    ISBN 0 521 57228 2 (hardback) 0 521 57643 1 (paperback)

31 H. E. Meller,
    Towns, Plans and Society in Modern Britain
    ISBN 0 521 57227 4 (hardback) 0 521 57644 X (paperback)

32 H. Hendrick,
    Children, Childhood and English Society, 1880–1990
    ISBN 0 521 57253 3 (hardback) 0 521 57624 5 (paperback)

33 N. Tranter,
    Sport, Economy and Society in Britain, 1750–1914
    ISBN 0 521 57217 7 (hardback) 0 521 57655 5 (paperback)

ISBN 0 521 57231 2 (hardback) 0 521 57640 7 (paperback)

47 A. Colli,
    Family Business in Historical and Comparative Perspective
    ISBN 0 521 80028 5 (hardback) 0 521 80472 8 (paperback)

Economic History Society

The Economic History Society, which numbers around 3,000 members, publishes the *Economic History Review* four times a year (free to members) and holds an annual conference. Enquiries about membership should be addressed to:

The Assistant Secretary
Economic History Society
PO Box 70
Kingswood
Bristol
BS15 5TB

Full-time students may join at special rates.